AF574451

Sad Friends, Drowned Lovers, Stapled Songs

Chard DeNiord

Sad Friends, Drowned Lovers, Stapled Songs:

Conversations and Reflections on Twentieth Century American Poets

Chard DeNiord

MARICK PRESS

Library of Congress Cataloguing in Publication Data

DeNiord, Chard
Sad Friends, Drowned Lovers, Stapled Songs
Non-Fiction
ISBN 978-1-934851-27-2

Design and typesetting by Really Big Robot
Cover design by Really Big Robot
Cover image: © Liz DeNiord, "November"; acrylic, 36" X 36"

Printed and bound in the United States

Marick Press
P.O. Box 36253
Grosse Pointe Farms
Michigan 48236
www.marickpress.com
Mariela Griffor, Publisher
Distributed by spdbooks.org
And Ingram

ACKNOWLEDGMENTS

AGNI: Interview with Donald Hall

Harvard Review: Sad Friend

Literary Imagination: Silence Amidst the Crowd,
A Reading of Philip Levine's "The Simple Truth"
and "Call It Music"

New England Review: The Place Where You Lie, A Reading of James Wright's "To the Muse"

American Poetry Review: Interviews with Jack Gilbert, Maxine Kumin, Ruth Stone, Galway Kinnell, Lucille Clifton, Robert Bly

I would like to thank the following people who were instrumental in the making of this book: Brett Corrigan, Maria Spellman, and Julie Strano for their long hours of transcribing, Ilya Kaminsky for his wise counsel to widen my range, Janet Masso for her administrative support, Providence College for its institutional support and generous CAFR grant, Marcia Croll, Alexia Clifton, Ruth Bly, Bobbie Kinnell, and Henry Lyman for their kindness and familial assistance, Liz deNiord for her support and encouragement throughout this undertaking, Alice Fogel for her proofreading and invaluable editorial counsel, Francesco Levato for his assiduous work in designing and formatting this book, and Mariela Griffor for her support and belief in this project.

CONTENTS

DEDICATION

In memory of Lucille Clifton

June 27, 1936 – February 13, 2010

i made it up
here on this bridge between
starshine and clay...

From "won't you celebrate with me" by Lucille Clifton

INTRODUCTION

Although the poets I chose to include in this book of interviews and essays represent only a cross section of notable post-war American poets, they nonetheless provide a window on their extraordinary generation of rebels who "yawped" from their rooftops with a daring presaged by Walt Whitman's prophetic challenge to future poets: "Leaving it to you to prove and define it, / Expecting the main things from you."

Manifesting an American spirit that embraced iconoclastic subject matter and styles, "meter making arguments" and the "main things," the poets in these interviews and essays—as well as others omitted by the practical limits of my initial undertaking to interview senior poets nationwide—ushered in a thrilling new era of American poetry that marked the fault-line between the last "whimper" of Modernism and what for the last fifty years has rather nebulously been called contemporary American poetry. As the last generation to come of age in the final days of the old world 12/5 work week in which both the daily and literary news were recorded on hard copy, these poets have not only survived their transition into the synchronic age of the Internet and 24/7 news cycle, but continued to add strength to strength in their new work.

These interviews took place over a three-year period from 2007 to 2010, with the exception of Jack Gilbert's two-part interview, which occurred in 2002 and 2006. During each interview, I was primarily interested in hearing these poets' reminiscences and views about their lives and careers, hoping our conversations would cover old ground in new ways. I was also interested in hearing their opinions about the differences and similarities between the present state of American poetry—its unprecedented big tent— and their own age that immediately preceded the cyber age, the proliferation of MFA programs, slam and performance competitions, desktop publishing, and writers' conventions. I was surprised but assured to hear from

Maxine Kumin that "it would all get sorted out in the end." Although so distinct from each other in their styles and aesthetics, these poets shared a few crucial traits, namely, a sedulous work ethic, ambivalence about fame, a love of solitude, a deep interest in hearing their poems read aloud, and an abiding interest in each other.

As a long-time reader and admirer of these poets, I was initially intimidated by the prospect of interviewing them. What, I wondered, could I ask them that dozens of previous interviewers hadn't already asked them? Not much. But I was pleasantly surprised by remarks they made, many in an off-handed manner that reflected a lifetime of honing their craft and expression. These included such revelations as Donald Hall's insight on the nature of human emotions: "No emotion is pure, but frequently we are aware of one and not the other. In poetry somehow you come out with both"; Galway Kinnell's epiphany on the value of art in relation to life: "Art is wonderful, but the moment love is smashed, darkness falls, deafness falls, nothing survives as it was"; Jack Gilbert's crystallized view on the difference between hubris and "real pride": "Real pride gives up; false pride keeps performing"; Robert Bly's redemptive belief in survival: "Each of us deserves to be forgiven. If only for 'our persistence in keeping our small boat afloat when so many have gone down in this world'"; Ruth Stone's startling admission: "Something funny, I can tell you, that when I'm writing I'm not experiencing anything…The writing is separate…I don't write out of the memory of experiencing a memory"; Maxine Kumin's recognition that her early poems of witness, especially those in *House, Bridge, Fountain, Gate* were more audacious than she realized: "I was not aware of it. Looking back they seem much more daring"; and Lucille Clifton's sagacious observation about her own writing rules: "I do carpentry that is needed for what's going on, in the carpenter's rule, not the poet's rule. One hopes to come ever closer to what poetry wants, what that poem wants."

At the conclusion of each interview, I felt I had just begun to explore the long, celebrated careers of each of my subjects. I asked several final questions, which all were most gracious in answering. But I left each one feeling I had really only skimmed the surface of their lives and careers, knowing that nothing I asked or anything they told me could ultimately substitute for the "memorable speech" and irreducible language of their poetry.

The fact that all these poets were still writing at the time I interviewed them testifies to their creative energy. As survivors of the Great Depression and World War II, they matured as poets throughout the second half of the twentieth century, feeling enormously empowered as members of a generation that had not only endured a decade of dire economic hardship, but also saved the world from fascism and tyranny. This confidence no doubt instilled them with a contagious subversiveness that compelled them to find their own new forms and subject matter—what Robert Bly called "the new imagination" in 1958—that would liberate American poets from the "mind forged manacles" of such national and cultural blights as McCarthyism, aesthetic jingoism, paternalism, racism, the Vietnam War, and gender discrimination. Each responded with his and her memorable answers, divining new language, strategies and voices that ushered in a post Modernist age that testified to the "aboriginal strength" of their genius, as well as to their chutzpah in believing that they could somehow accomplish the impossible of "making new" in the wake of their formidable Modernist predecessors.

These poets, in a departure from the Modernists' mostly New Critical aesthetic, implicated themselves and their families in their poems in personal, political and aesthetic ways, taking Whitman's song of the self to new transpersonal heights that obviated the first person myths of their confessional peers—Sylvia Plath, Anne Sexton, W.D. Snodgrass, John Berryman, Robert Lowell—in favor of the sublime other of child, sibling, parent, stranger, river, bear, soldier, war victim, beloved etc. New blood streamed through the lines of their groundbreaking books in the sixties and seventies, specifically Galway Kinnell's *What a Kingdom It Was* (1960), Robert Bly's *Silence in the Snowy Fields* (1962), Maxine Kumin's *Up Country* (1973), Jack Gilbert's *Views of Jeopardy* (1962), Ruth Stone's *In an Iridescent Time* (1959); Lucille Clifton's *good times* (1969) and Donald Hall's *Kicking the Leaves* (1978). Although innovative in their forms and subject matter, they maintained a strong adherence to clarity and sense, a coherence that would continue to resonate in their work well into the first decade of this century when "making sense" hasn't always been an aesthetic priority. This sense-making, however, has taken its psychic toll on these poets, a not always so public repercussion of their individual struggles as citizens, family members and artists. In his poem "Pure Balance" (from his 2006 book *Strong Is Your Hold*) for instance, Galway Kinnell declares with plangent concision that "Clarity/ turns out to be/ an invisible form of sadness." This humanizing "sadness" permeates all these poets' work in both recrudescent and refined language that stands as an essential witness of the last half of the twentieth century. And yet complementing this legacy of sadness are also ecstatic moments for which they have paid, in the words of Emily Dickinson, with an "anguish…in keen and quivering ratio to the ecstasy." Indeed, they lived in interesting times, but they were instrumental in making their time interesting by defining it memorably in ways that were at once particular and transcendent, personal and political, plain and poetic.

–Chard DeNiord

Interviews

JACK GILBERT

Photo by Robert Tobey

The first part of this two part interview took place at New England College on July 10th, 2003 during a two day visit Jack Gilbert made to the New England College MFA program's summer residency. Li Young Lee and Carrie Collins, Jack's partner at the time, were also present during this interview that took place in the dorm room where Jack was staying.

The second part of this interview took place at Henry Lyman's house in Northampton, Mass. where Jack lived from 2000 to 2009. Jack emerged from his room shortly after I arrived appearing frail and thin and sat on a couch in front of a picture window that looked onto a deep gulch that descended sharply behind Henry Lyman's house. He greeted me in a voice that was barely louder than a whisper and asked me where I wanted "to pick up," as if aware three years later of exactly where we had left off. I read the last part of his first interview back to him and then proceeded to ask him my first question, noticing, however, as I turned to push the record button on my tape recorder that I had left the machine's electrical cord at home. Rather than interrupt the interview, I decided to start transcribing our conversation as if nothing were amiss. Fortunately, Jack neither noticed that my tape recorder wasn't on or that I was writing down everything he said in long hand. He simply spoke in a clear, soft voice just slowly enough for me to transcribe his every word. After fifteen minutes or so of proceeding like this, I was so absorbed in what he was saying that I hardly noticed I was writing at all.

Part I

CD: Jack, your poems have so much human presence and pressure in them. Do you achieve this by working on the poems or by living your life? Or both?

JG: I don't write poems as a way of writing a poem. I think I'm more prone to writing a poem on something I think I see or know or understand that is new. It's like what I've I said about having an illicit relationship. It's not a question of cheating on somebody or wanting to get laid, or seeking physical pleasure. But for whatever reason there is this illicit relationship. If you've ever experienced that, caring about a man or woman in an illicit way, there's an emotional quality in that apartment that doesn't exist any other place in the world. I'm not saying it's good or bad. That sadness, that knowledge that this can't last, that you're hurting someone too much, the poem tries to capture this, this great tenderness. Maybe I'm playing with somebody else's baby so she can do the cooking. There's an intimacy in that illegitimacy that I think is unique, if the people are serious with each other. I want to confront death in my poetry. Like in the lines I read last night from my poem "A Brief for the Defense." "Sorrow everywhere. Slaughter everywhere. If babies/ aren't starving someplace, they are starving/ someplace else. With flies in their nostrils./ But we enjoy our lives because that's what God wants." We must not let misery take away our happiness. It's a crazy thing to say because life can be horrifying. We live in a world that has death in it, and injustice and all these things. But it's important to go on being capable of happiness or delight in the world, not to ignore these other things, but to recognize that we have to build our poems within a bad terrain. It's just how life is.

CD: Yes, but what I'm amazed by is how you bring that reality, that life, into a poem, and also how you wed your craft of such spare, lyrical lines to what Matthew Arnold called "high seriousness." [This first question was suggested to me by Li-Young Lee.]

JG: To get the technicalities straight, so the form is done right, simple, all the technicalities, I think that's a waste of time. It's nice. But that's not what great poetry is. I think one of the main things is simply concrete detail. After all, speaking is one of the newer arts of human beings. Seeing is infinitely older. We react from seeing something much more than we react from hearing it said. We are designed to respond to physicality. Like in basketball game, the man is going shoot the ball to win the game, is standing there doing nothing at the line. Now what he is doing often is visualizing himself taking the ball, making it bounce in his hand, lifting the muscle, shooting, watching it go up and up, and down and down and in the basket. When he does that, then his body can sense, Oh, I can do that! And I can imitate that! If you tell me an abstraction then, it's no good. It may or not get through. Draw me a picture, make a movie, and let me see. Then I think that's what the large thing with poetry is. It's not all of it. It's one of the big parts. The concreteness. That's why abstraction, like with modern experimentalists and post-modern theorists, they don't have any feelings anymore. Why it's abstract. It's not human and therefore it can't have an emotional impact on the human reading the book, and therefore the person reading does not experience the things we talked about. At least that's how I see it. And if it's not going to have an emotional impact on the reader, that's ok, but I'm not interested.

CD: Why do you think people are writing this way today? What do you feel happened?

JG: One of the things I suspect is that people mistrust feeling, in so many ways. In addition to that, the poets of today came after a golden age in American poetry with T.S. Eliot, William Carlos Williams, Wallace Stevens and Ezra Pound. It seems to me that the next generations of poets had to become experimentalists to make a place for themselves, to do something different after those four giants. Those poets did their thing and a new generation came along after them and they wanted to do their thing, but now they have to chop down all the trees to make a space to grow their garden. Unfortunately they haven't been able to raise a good crop. Much of postmodern poetry has no significance at all. Unless you like puzzles. Unless you can figure out what the thing is about. The point is not to mystify the reader but to trick the reader into feeling something, knowing something This whole absurdity about doubting the 'I' in poetry I don't understand at all. That's the source of communication of things that matter. At least, that's what I feel. I want to trust the speaker of the poem. It's like biting into gold, to see if it's true metal. Poets work by insight, not by cleverness. If not through inspiration, then through intuition. Not by mechanics or examining the nature of the way someone seeing something encounters something. In much postmodern poetry the eyeball follows a certain little trail and then translates what it sees back into something else, proclaiming then, "Yes that is a dog." What the hell good is that? If you're scientifically inclined, it's wonderful. It's an extraordinary science of cognition, but it's nothing that has anything to do with my life emotionally, and if its not emotional what does it offer? It can offer beauty, perhaps, if you're interested in that. It's nice, but it's not going to change your life. Telling a story is very nice, but unless the thing, the novel, the short story does something to you as a person, then its just another artifact. It may be pretty, it may be clever, causing you to say, "Oh, that was ingenious. I wouldn't have thought it was going to come out that way."

CD: Can you give me an example of a poem or a book of poems that changed your life in some way?

JG: The first influence on my poetry was ancient Chinese poetry-Li Po, Tu Fu--because it had this extraordinary ability to make me experience the emotional thing the poets were feeling, and doing it with no means. I was fascinated by that: how much you could do with so little. It's cumulative in a novel. You can do it by having 280 days of tales as an illusion of reality. What's his name, I forget it now, the guy who wrote Little Nell. He wrote stories for the newspaper in installments and finally he came to the place where he had to kill off Little Nell and he couldn't make himself do it, and he said to himself, "Now it's up. You have to do it." Finally one night, he gathered himself together and wrote down the thing and Little Nell died. He walked the streets of London all night with tears running down his face. That's art to me.

CD: So the change involves a deepening of your feelings, what Emily Dickinson called "the internal difference, where the meanings are."

JG: Your actual being is changed. My heart, for instance, was partially made by the songs of Frank Sinatra and by movies I went to when I was growing up. My heart was shaped by stories, by pictures, by songs. I believe we are made by art, art that matters. Not what's ingenious, clever, or hard to do. Not a mystery puzzle. I think if a poem doesn't put pressure on me, I don't feel uncomfortable in the sense of feeling more than I can feel, understanding more than I can understand, loving more than I am able to be in love. It enables me to do those things. If you try to copy an image and everything goes right, you may feel like more of a person afterwards. But I think that work of art is probably a failure. It's nice to put a novel on paper, a painting over the couch. But I don't want it unless it's significant, unless it has something to do with me. If it's just clever or entertaining or surprising, it's a waste of time for me. I enjoy it. I do it. I read the novel, you know, the simple story line behind a mystery of who killed the cat. That's entertaining, but that's not what I think poetry is about. I think it's something about putting pressure on me. If it doesn't put pressure on the reader, what's it for.

CD: I have heard that you have several hundred uncollected and unpublished poems lying around your house. Do you plan to publish these poems?

JG: That's right. I'm not sure what I intend to do with them.

CD: Why?

JG: Well there are several reasons. One is, I've never had much impulse to publish. I waited 14 years between my first and second book. Ten years between my second and third book. I love to write poetry, and I love to get it right. Sometimes I'm a workaholic, getting it to where I think it's right. But, I guess one of the things is that I don't believe in poetry today, because it's involved with money so much, and careerism I don't believe people would continue to write poetry, most of them, if there was no money to be made in poetry. You don't make money directly in poetry, but if you get noticed you get jobs in colleges, things like that. Then you can buy a house and raise a nice family so you can be proud of yourself. But I don't like that use of poetry. I love it, and still love it, in my memory, when there was no money to be made in poetry. When nobody could make money off poetry.

CD: But perhaps you're hiding your light under a bushel basket.

JG: Well it's not going to change anybody's life.

CD: You just said that a good poem changes a person's life!

JG: Absolutely.

CD: And you write good poems.

JG: Yes, but that doesn't mean I have to do it all of the time.

CD: Every ten or fourteen years?

JG: Yes.

CD: The MFA students were deeply moved by your reading last night.

JG: That's impressive. When I give a reading I'm surprised at the people who take it seriously because we live in an age of entertainment. Today's children grow up on electronic games, sports, and other things. But I think generally there isn't time to take things seriously nowadays. I'm not bitter about it. I don't feel like it's sour grapes because I'm lucky enough that I can publish what I publish. But I don't know what you're going to do about the fact that the audience for poetry today is basically not there, unless you're writing a kind of puzzle that gives people a rush of happiness in solving it.

CD: There's a young woman in the program who was thinking about leaving yesterday. She confessed that she was terrified of taking herself seriously as a poet. She approached me about an hour ago to tell me that she had decided to remain in the program. I asked her why and she said because of your reading last night. That was the only reason she gave.

JG: Bless her. That's a very nice thing that you told me.

CD: And because of Jack Gilbert's poems that she heard last night for the first time. She's twenty one years old and she's been brought up on electronic games. She's a reader also.

JG: How do you explain the fact that poetry has changed so much? It seems to me that a lot of people want to be poets; they want to be poets for a very human reason; they want to get recognition, and if there's no recognition, I think there would be a few poets. There'd be a few, perhaps, but not many. I hate to say it, but its true, at these writing conferences it's all about fixing up a poem so it will sell. Nobody wants to talk about how a poem works, what its purpose is. They all want to deal with the outside of the poem. Does it look good? Should I take the left line out and put it over here? How should I make the rhythm correct and such. But hardly anybody talks about the strategies of poetry, or how you make poetry live, how to use concrete detail rather than similes, goddamned similes, the weakest kind of resource there is in poetry. People are so much in love with similes. It's a pity. The mechanics of poetry have little to do with design. There's no pressure, it seems to me, to write poems that matter today. Everybody wants to write poems that will be celebrated, but that doesn't mean that they matter. Poetry has changed my life and I think it's changed other peoples' lives. I don't see it changing people's life today.

CD: Because of the recent failures of poetry? Because of video games? Because of careerism? Because of MFA programs?

JG: All of those are true, and should be dealt with, but poets can't afford to be so delicate. You have to succeed in the midst of corruption and wanting to write poetry because you want to be admired, so that you will be able to have more girlfriends or something like that. That's human. That's not what worries me, it makes me mad, but it doesn't worry me. What makes me worry is that they don't know why they are writing poetry. What's the reason to write poetry? It's not a hobby. It's one of the major ways of keeping the world human. We have almost nothing else, no craft that deals specifically with feeling. The novel to some extent, but it embodies a different kind of empathy than a poem does, and I suppose film to a degree, but motion pictures are only able to show you the outside of what's happening. Poetry works on the inside of what's happening.

CD: That is the state of things, but if we had more of your poems wouldn't that be a service to the world?

JG: That's not a fair way to argue.

CD: Why not? Wouldn't it provide an invaluable cultural and social service, as your reading did last night for the students, faculty and guests?

JG: Well I think it came about when poetry got mixed up with money and fame, and such. I didn't come from that kind of background. As I said about ancient Chinese poetry, and it's the same with ancient Greek poetry, it's not because of its historical value per se, but because its value as great art. Somebody once said writing poems is a bastard art, a queenly profession. But it's not like that now. There's a cheapness to so much poetry. I would like to see a moratorium on poetry for twenty five years and see how many people are writing poems, seriously. I think you would have about a dozen left.

CD: You once said that Greek sailors don't play on the beach and I don't write funny poetry.

JG: Right. That's nice. That's one of the reasons to publish. Someone quotes a poem to you on the street and it turns out to be yours.

CD: But I sense there is an underlying current of humor in a lot of your poetry and without it you wouldn't be able to be as serious as you are,

JG: I hope it's there. Its' just like you need short poems and long poems. You need happy poems and unhappy poems. You need a variety of poetry. Humor is particularly like a poem for lovers. "When I hear people talk about how passionate/ they are, I think of two cleaning ladies/ at a second-story window watching a man/ coming back from a party where there was/ lots of free beer. He runs in and out/ of buildings looking for a toilet. 'My lord,'/ the tall woman says, 'that fellow down there surely loves architecture.'"

CD: From your poem "Lovers." I also think your poem "Going Wrong" concludes on a various humorous note. "Take out the fish/ and scrambled eggs. I am not stubborn, he thinks,/ laying all of it on the table in the courtyard/ full of early sun, shadows of swallows

flying/ on the food. Not stubborn, just greedy."
JG: It's also very nice to hear from somebody else. Yeah, I laugh a lot.

CD: Well this student deciding to stay here in this program instead of going to law school that's a very physical, real change.

JG: Well it's wonderful and so flattering. It's great to hear. I went to a reading several years ago and after it was over-this is going to sound pompous-several people who knew I was in the audience came over to me and formed a circle, which was good for my vanity. I'm saying this ironically. Then suddenly a man in his early forties, maybe his late thirties, just an ordinary guy, came pushing through this group that had formed me, and without saying hello or introducing himself, said, "I want you to know that you've been keeping me alive with your poetry since 1982." Without giving me time to respond, he pushed his way to the other side and disappeared. I never could find him. But that was deeply moving.

Part II

CD: Jack, I know I've asked you this three years ago, but I wonder if you could elaborate a bit further on why you waited so long to publish between each of your four books.

JG: I didn't want to immerse myself in the poetry world, to fight those battles, to argue and argue.

CD: Why did you start writing poetry in the first place? Do your family read poetry and encourage you to write it?

JG: I don't come from any background. My parents were farmers. My father ran away from home when he was young to become a circus performer.

CD: So what interested you about poetry as a child and young man?

JG: My mind was just so fixed on understanding. I had a huge appetite to understand.

CD: Many of your poems appear to turn on fine ironic points. I'm thinking of such lines as "What we feel most has/ no name but amber, archers, cinnamon, horses and birds" from "The Forgotten Dialect of the Heart," as if to say there really are names for those things we feel most but they must be expressed as synecdoches, or the concluding lines from "Voices Inside and Out": "'Less and less,' I think./ The Brazilians say, 'In this country we have everything/ we need, except what we don't have.," which is such a sharp litotes, or those wonderful paradoxical lines from "The Great Fires": "Love lasts by not lasting." But you've also proclaimed in your poem "The Abnormal Is Not Courage" this straightforward Platonic aspiration, "The real form. The culmination. And the exceeding./ Not the surprise. The amazed understanding. The marriage,/ not the month's rapture. Not the exception. The beauty/ that is of many days. Steady and clear./ It is the normal excellence, of long accomplishment." Such sentiment appears to belie any overriding ironic intent in your work.. Do you view irony as a necessary function of a poetic dialectic in which your expression shifts back and forth between direct and ironic speech?

JG: Irony is the wrong word. It's almost insulting. All irony is this way for me. I was always interested in attaining a clarity and logic in which reason won out over decoration. There's always the danger of making something clearer than it is. Of course I'm interested in writing about complex things, but I recognize the danger of being too clever in doing this.

CD: How do you feel you have safeguarded yourself against cleverness?

JG: I love it, and I love vanity. It's one reason I gave up giving readings. I got so good at it, I felt I could control an audience.

CD: Why did grow so wary of your talent for reading so well?

JG: I would like to think I was really smart at seeing my weaknesses.

CD: Which were?

JG: My pride and my strength.

CD: Why do feel your pride and strength were also your weaknesses?

JG: I came to see what performance does to someone. It rots you. You become so vain. This is why I refuse to give readings. Because I am weak, it's hard to resist the power.. You're like an actor who can capture the audience with your words, your style, your appearance.

CD: Then where does your real power come from?

JG: I don't trust myself. I love the effect so much. It's like if you have the power to make women fall in love with you. I don't want to become that person, that performer, that figure who can intoxicate his audience. If II wanted to I could make a lot of money. But then I wouldn't want to give it up.

CD: What is the power in you to resist the power?

JG: I would like to think it's the strength of real pride.

CD: How do you distinguish real pride from false pride?

JG: Real pride gives up, false pride keeps performing.

CD: How do you feel now in looking back on your life, your career?

JG: Grateful. I lived my life so richly in so many ways. By falling in love. By being poor. I lived my life in such a wide range of being me. Not deliberately, but that's the way it happened. I've had an extraordinary life.

CD: How many times have you fallen in love?

JG: Three times. But there is another way of falling in love. There's the pleasure of just being close to a woman. It's interesting the range of being in love before it turns to pleasure. I've been so lucky. it's like when you reach the time of dying-a feeling of gratitude that' you've had all the life there was for you. It's hard for me not to feel content because when I was fifteen and realized death, believing still in God at that time, I said to myself, "I know God can take me, but not before I've had my life." I spent that year making a list of those things I wanted, starting with love, having a physical relationship,. Among my books and all those things, there are lists of what I wanted first. And I don't feel now there are any of the important things I missed. There's still sorrow because you lose a lot, but at least you're still there. It was not vanity for vanity's sake, or pleasure, but for what was important. I lived all my dreams. I feel so lucky and grateful because I don't believe in God, so I don't have anyone to thank. For me, it's just the pleasure of realizing how much I was able to have.

CD: You know what's missing here-any talk about your poems or your life as a poet.

JG: Oh, that was maybe seventh on my list.

CD: Why was that? You seem to have pursued your life with what Kierkegaard called "a purity of heart in willing one thing," namely poetry.

JG: Because that feels about right.

CD: You've put most of your time into poetry? Why then is it so far down your list of things you wished for most out of life?

JG: What's better than that? My other priorities have prevented me from becoming rich, vain and unhappy. It's because I'm greedy, the other things, wealth and fame, aren't sufficient. They disappear.

CD: So what doesn't disappear?

JG: Love, access to my life, access to people. I love being myself, to experience what there was in my life. The thing that always frightened me was to miss the important things, not from the eyes of the world, but from my eyes, my heart, my experience.

CD: But wasn't poetry a vital exercise for you in finding enduring expression about those things that meant most to you?

JG: Sometimes I think I write poetry for vanity.

CD: I would like to read you your poem "Tear It Down" and get your response in light of what you've just said about vanity:

TEAR IT DOWN

We find out the heart only by dismantling what
the heart knows. By redefining the morning,
we find a morning that comes just after darkness.
We can break through marriage into marriage.
By insisting on love we spoil it, get beyond
affection and wade mouth-deep into love.
We must unlearn the constellations to see the stars.
But going back toward childhood will not help.
The village is not better than Pittsburgh.
Only Pittsburgh is more than Pittsburgh.
Rome is better than Rome in the same way the sound
of raccoon tongues licking the inside walls
of the garbage tub is more than the stir
of them in the muck of the garbage. Love is not
enough. We die and are put into the earth forever.
We should insist while there is still time. We must
eat through the wildness of her sweet body already
in our bed to reach the body within that body.

JG: That's very nice to hear.

CD: Do you feel this was written out of vanity?

JG: Yes, but also more a delight. What moves me is hearing what I've done.

CD: You write in this poem, "Only Pittsburgh is more than Pittsburgh" and "Rome is better than Rome." Do you feel is some curious way that Jack Gilbert is better than Jack Gilbert when he's writing?

JG: Yes, sure, but I take that for granted. It's like coming across a piece of grass. It's just a pleasure. It's manifest in front of me.

CD: So you feel like a witness that transcends yourself.

JG: I just feel lucky. I don't feel like I own it. I made it, but that's different. It's more about the pleasure that's just there when it's done, whether anyone sees it or not. I see it myself, quietly. I'm not showing anyone.

CD: So you have a very large but selfless sense of your own audience?

JG: Yes.

CD: This selfless awareness reminds me of Ivan Ilych's death-bed epiphany in Tolstoy's story "The Death of Ivan Ilych." Ivan struggles to ask for forgiveness from his wife, but in his weakness utters "forgo" instead of "forgive," knowing in the end that it doesn't matter if he's understood.

JG: That's a very nice way to say it. I have so much gratitude and I don't have any regret for it. My gratitude is very simple in this way.

CD: You must get up in the morning feeling very happy.

JG: Yes, most of the time, but I'm also very angry about aging, about not being able anymore to do things I want to do. I don't bother myself about the loss. I feel it, and the anger diminishes. So much has been given to me.

CD: I remember you once telling me when you lived with my wife and me in Iowa for a few months that many poets of your reputation and prestige enjoy flying on planes and going places, but that you're content just to stare out the window of the Greyhound bus.

JG: Yes. I like my memories of being hungry and lost. I relish all those things. The experience of being myself. To be privileged to have been there, in my life.

CD: Like a guest of yourself?

JG: Not a guest, but to have had it.

MAXINE KUMIN

Photo by John Hession

Maxine greeted me at her front door and invited me into her kitchen on the day of our scheduled interview, March 15, 2009. I had visited her socially several times during the years she worked at the New England College MFA Program in Poetry in Henniker, New Hampshire, so I was familiar with her hillside horse farm and rambling country house known as Pobiz in Warner, New Hampshire. We sat at her kitchen table and began talking right away about her life in the Pobiz. Never one for small talk or mere polite conversation, Maxine proceeded to reflect on her career, her family and friends, and her poems with clarity, frankness and zest. The time passed quickly as we jumped back and forth between the events of her life and the arc of her career as a poet. Maxine had notified me when I arrived at nine that her vet had scheduled an appointment with one of her elderly sick horses at noon. I had lost track of time in the midst of the interview and was surprised to hear the vet's knock at the door after what seemed like only an hour. Maxine announced to me that it was in fact noon. I was reminded again that Maxine's attention to time and details had always been sharper than mine, in both her poems and the daily business. As she bid me farewell, I realized as I stood in her driveway gazing at the horses in her field that Maxine's writing life was an integral part of her larger life—her family, her marriage to Victor, her horses, her garden, her swimming pond, her environmental and political causes—and that one complemented the other in organic ways that were essential to each other, whether quotidian and private or literary and public.

CD: Your poems have become increasingly confident, bold and courageous, without losing their lyrical power. Rather than showing any signs of flaming out as you enter your eighth decade, as many poets often do, you have sustained your signature candor and craft in your most recent books Jack and Still to Mow. You take admirable risks with the rendition and torture poems that are remarkable for their witness to Bush's and Rumsfeld's abrogation of constitutional tenets and basic human rights. I'm hard-pressed to think of many younger women and men writing today with the same political vocabulary. With the same confidence about the poetry of witness.

MK: When Galway Kinnell introduced me at a reading I gave recently at the Atheneum in St. Johnsbury, Vermont I was struck when he said much the same thing about those poems. I think I've been praised and damned in equal measure for the so-called torture poems, so to have him choose them for singular praise really touched me. And it is true that at this point in my life I feel that I have nothing to lose. I'm not thinking in terms of reputation or next book. I'm just writing what is wrung from me.

CD: Even though you've already written so many poems about your horses and farm life, do you feel these subjects continue to provide a rich source of inspiration for you?

MK: I'm still writing an awful lot of poems about my animals. I have an old broodmare who is supposed to be dying, and I've just written two more poems about her.

CD: Do you see any connection between your public poems of witness and your domestic, pastoral poems?

MK: The poems I am speaking of now, about the horses and dogs are poetry of witness in their own way.

CD: How would you say you cross that boundary, between the pastoral and the political?

MK: Well to me, my so-called animal poems, for instance, are truly political. We've been in the rescue business for about 40 years and this little dog that you just met is our newest waif. She came up from Tennessee in April from a horrible life, unspeakable life, and we were told we could never let her loose because she would run and run and never be seen again. And here she is, totally at liberty.

CD: Yes.

MK: We've rescued a number of dogs and we've also rescued several horses.

CD: That's witnessing on a whole other front.

MK: I seem unable to keep them out of my work. Imagine writing two sonnets about dogs. "Xochi's Tale," which is in *Still to Mow*, is about our dog Xochi who unfortunately died last October and in April we took in Rosie. She came with a grade three or four heart murmur, so she's on medication. We didn't know her age but our vet says she's ten years old. If you could see her streaking across the pastures and trotting on top of the stone walls, I think you'd agree that if she drops dead tomorrow she will have had a life.

CD: Your poems of witness, whether they're about Iraq, Cheney, your dogs or your horses emanate from a strong compassion that you have in the face of enormous obstacles. I heard yesterday that the government plans to kill 3,500 mustangs in Nevada because they don't know what to do with all of these horses. Have you heard this?

MK: It's an old sad story. It's because they've given all of the grazing rights to cattle. The Bureau of Land Management leases it to farmers for pennies per acre and the land cannot sustain wild horses and all the meat that we seem to feel we have to eat. Don't get me started.

CD: Just as you've always kept watch on such national issues as cruelty to animals, human torture and environmental pollution, you've also always kept your hands busy in your own soil.

MK: Yes, you should see my vegetable garden. I'll take you up.

CD: I would love to. You have a green thumb, as well as a tireless love for dogs and horses.

MK: I apparently came with this tireless love because when I was a child I was always bringing something home and saying, "He followed me can I keep him?"

CD: Your early poems are remarkable in the way they move from your questions of selfhood in 1942 through 1945 to finding your voice as a poet during a time of powerful new expression among other women poets, particularly Ann Sexton and Sylvia Plath in the late fifties and early sixties.. There is a courage and rawness in your voice, but also an abiding quality. You used that word, "abiding," in your poem "Morning Swim," which shows a patience…

MK: A stubbornness.

CD: In your poem "The Pawn Broker," you express an implicit stubbornness as you strive to create your own nascent identity as a young poet. You refer to your father as “a man of great personal order.” You credit him with teaching you “a love ingrown, tight as an oyster.” The stanza in which this line appears in “The Pawn Broker” evinces the “ingrown” love you claim as both your inheritance and lesson from your father, and the exquisite jewel it produced. “Firsthand I had from my father a love ingrown/ tight as an oyster, and returned it/ as secretly. From him firsthand/ the grace of work, the sweat of it, the bone-/ tired unfolding down from stress./ I was the bearer he paid up on demand/ With one small pearl of selfhood. Portionless,/ I am oystering still to earn it.”

MK:. I didn’t write them out of anger, as you suggested before. Actually I worshipped my father, but he was the autocrat. There’s no question about it.

CD: In your poem “Life’s Work” from *House, Bridge, Fountain, Gate*, you eulogize your father as a member of the patriarchal past. “Well, the firm old fathers are dead,” you write, “and I didn’t come to grief.”

MK: Right

CD: But you did come to words, as you go on to say in the same poem. “I came to words instead,/ to tell the little tale that’s left:/ the midnights of my childhood still go on.” You downplay your heroic narrative by calling it a “little tale” and you deftly describe your mother’s oppressive life in haunting, musical lines that close the poem. “The stairs speak again under your foot,/ the heavy parlor door folds shut/ and Claire de Lune/ puckers from the obedient keys/ plain as a schoolroom clock ticking/ and what I hear more clearly than Debussy’s/ lovesong is the dry aftersound/ of your long nails clicking.”

MK: Well, my mother was a prisoner. She was a captive of her upwardly mobile yearnings.

CD: That's quietly angry. No wonder you had that attachment. But just that image, the clicking of your mother's fingernails in "Life's Work" conveying her pent-up frustration at not being able to pursue a career of her own certainly evokes a powerful sense of her entrapment and frustration.

MK: I have to confess it took me a very long time to appreciate her entrapment. I see her plight now. She was a captive of her time and place and she was so desperately anxious to rise from the ranks, as it were. A social position of some eminence, that was so important to her. And she had her piano.

CD: That was all she could hold on to.

MK: And her manicured fingernails.

CD: But she was an aspiring musician.

MK: At one time she was.

CD. And she apparently had fallen in love with some other musician?

MK: No, she simply wanted to be his accompanist and her father forbade her to travel with him.

CD: I see, I didn't know if he was her lover.

MK: No, he was an older man.

CD: But the way this elegy ends- your mother "buried without her corset but in silk"- makes a sad commentary on not only her, but most of the women of her generation's unrealized dreams.

MK: That was the figure she fought for. How far away that seems to me, that life. The hats and gloves in order to go downtown.

MK: It took me along time to come to terms with my mother because I was never the popular outgoing daughter that she intended.

CD: And your father?

MK: Well, I don't know about my father. He thought I could do anything. I think the crowning moment was when my first book came out just a year before he died. I don't think…I doubt that he ever read it, but at least he held it in his hands and he could say, "My daughter is a writer." And that was sacred, you know?

CD: There's also that wonderful poem about your attempt to become a communist at Radcliffe.

MK: Yes (laughing). Well, that was my one moment of open rebellion, telling him to go ahead and try to yank me out of Radcliffe. I'm staying no matter what. I'll get a scholarship and a work-study job and hang on. He backed right down and we never discussed it again.

CD: Right, but then you also left those friends.

MK: I did, I didn't have the courage to continue going out at 6 a.m. to organize for the CIO at the Fore River Shipyard. It was 1942, you might say ironically that it was my contribution to the war effort. The funny thing is I look at some of these people, one of them was my friend Bobby Lewis, we took accelerated Russian together, two Cliffies in a group of army privates learning Russian in the student training program. and I see what traditional citizens we turned out to be. She married Bob Solow, who went on to win a Nobel prize in economics. She was about as red as you can get. Another one of that group of us picketing the shipyard is now a professor at Harvard.

CD: Is it really true the FBI went down to your father and told him your daughter was consorting with communists?

MK: Yes, absolutely true.

CD: There is a lot of family history in your early poems, which are beautifully narrated, but they are also lyrical in just the right spots. Would you go so far as to call these poems "confessional"?

MK: Well, it depends on your definition of confessional. My poems were certainly autobiographical, so that qualifies them in one sense as confessional.

CD: Your poems "Sperm," The Thirties Revisited" and "Heaven is Anus," all from *House, Bridge, Fountain, Gate* in 1975 are further evidence of the marriage of your public and confessional muses. This voice's double duty is strongly evident in such lines from "The Thirties Revisited" as, "Soon enough the uncles will give thanks/ for GI uniforms to choose/ and go off tough as terriers to dig their holes./ Warsaw will excrete its last Jews." And then a few line later you shift without losing a beat to this remarkable private adolescent scene with you and your mother, moving from the world on the verge of bloody war to your own personal bleeding. “This is the year that mother stiffens./ She undresses in the closet giving me/ her back as if I can’t see/ her breasts fall down like pufferfish,/ the life gone out of their crusty eyes,/ But who has punctured the bathroom light?/ Why does the mattress moan at night/ and why is nothing good/ said of all the business to come/-the elastic belt with its metal tongue-/when my body, that surprise,/ claps me into my first blood.?” It seems you have been writing poems of witness all along. Are you aware of this?

MK: I was not aware of it. Looking back they seem much more daring.

CD: They were daring. A stanza like this for instance from “Sperm,” which you wrote in the early seventies, is still daring: ‘Oh grandfather, what is it saying,/ these seventeen cousins-german/ descending the same number of steps/ their chromosomes tight as a chain gang/ their genes like innocent porters/ a milk churn of spermatozoa? You have to admire the product--/bringing forth sons to be patriots/ daughters to dance like tame puppets--/ half of them dead or not speaking/ while Sukey and James, the end of the line/ keep house in the gentlest tradition/ of spinster and bachelor sweetheart.”

MK: Yes.

CD: “The product” you call it?

MK: That led me ultimately to Wordsworth and Dorothy. That’s a subject that has fascinated me for years.

CD: You've written about them three or four times. Do you know what the fascination is exactly?

MK: It was serendipitous. I just stumbled on Dorothy Wordsworth's journals from their time together at Grassmere. I bought that book and I couldn't put it down.

CD: Have you been to Grasmere?

MK: No.

CD: I was surprised by how spare and primitive Wordsworth's house was.

MK: No wonder he went into the woods to alter his poems. He didn't have a decent study. And he walked everywhere. They were too poor to have horses, so they walked.

CD: Well, that's the first thing I thought when I was there, the poverty.

MK: And there Dorothy was toiling in the garden, picking peas and tying up the scarlet runner beans.

CD: What was it about their relationship that fascinates you?

MK: Even for its time it seemed odd. More than odd...I don't know if their relationship was incest or not. They lived together for seven years, and then he took her to France to meet his mistress, and then she couldn't go to his wedding because she was afraid she would ruin it by weeping. And he gave her the wedding ring to wear the day before the wedding. I mean, what does that tell you?

CD: That it was a little incestuous.

MK: A little?

CD: Very?

MK: So, maybe that's what must have fascinated me way back when I started to write about all these cousins. "Sperm" and "The Thirties Revisited" are part truth, part invention.

CD: You were both personally and poetically immersed in the era of Confessionalism in the sixties and early seventies through your own writing but also through your close friendship with Anne Sexton. In Conradian terms, it seems you were to Anne Sexton as Marlow was to Kurtz. Did you ever get a clear sense of the darkness she was looking into, and if so, how did that awareness affect your own work?

MK: Well, of course, I had a very strong sense of the darkness she was looking into. There were probably six or seven attempted suicides over the seventeen years of our enduring friendship and some of the early ones perhaps were staged, but before I ever met her she had tried seriously to take her own life. She had a severe postpartum depression.

CD: Yes, and she suffered from bipolar disorder as well.

MK: The terminology is just that– naming something little

understood. While I had a strong sense of the darkness she was looking into, but I don't know that it…it's a funny thing. We were able somehow to have a close relationship, an intense personal relationship.

CD: You won the Pulitzer Prize for *Up Country* which contains many persona poems in the voice of Henry the hermit. You said you thought people were more likely to read poems in a man's voice than in a woman's. But Sexton and Plath had already proven otherwise by the time *Up Country* was published. Many poems in *Privilege* and *The Nightmare Factory* address the same familial and personal topics that Plath and Sexton had written about, but it's not until *House, Bridge, Fountain, Gate* that you really delve into a recrudescent mode in poems such as "Sperm," "The Thirties Revisited," "Heaven as Anus," "Life's Work," "The Jesus Infection," "Song for Seven Parts of the Body." Were you emboldened by Anne to write some of these poems, especially after her death?

MK: I can't say for sure, but I don't think I was emboldened by the Sexton and Plath poems. Somehow Anne and I were able to energize the process of writing by listening to each other's starts and false starts, but we were each absolutely singular in voice and intent. This was conscious though largely unspoken between us. If we intruded on each other's work, it would be, as I see it, that my diction freshened, I began to avoid Latinate constructions, unnecessary adjectives, and began to develop a more muscular vocabulary. What I brought to Anne's works was the reliance on form, on rhyme and off-rhyme, especially as ways to deal with such heavily confessional poems as "Cripples and Other Stories," which was literally in the wastebasket until I urged her to take it out and pound it into form. The recrudescence you speak of in the poems in *House, Bridge,*

Fountain, Gate onward I think merely represents my increasing faith in myself as I grew as a poet. If these are more daring, more overt, it is because I felt I now had some stature and could tackle these themes. As for the hermit and Henry poems, I really did not think a female hermit would carry the weight of my invented male. And Henry was, after all, Henry. Much of what I wrote about him was true. Some was invented. He was our neighbor at the foot of the hill. Of course that house crumbled and fell in almost while he was living in it, but the people who bought the property built a house on exactly that footprint. I didn't have a title for that book. Anne had been writing the fairytale poems, and she said, "Well, I don't know. What shall I call them?" And then I said, "You can call them 'Transformations'." And then she looked at my manuscript which was lacking a title and she said, "Well, you're always talking about going 'up country' every weekend. Call the book '*Up Country*'."

When Anne killed herself in October of 1974, I felt for a long time that the "fun" had gone out of writing poems. The fun of sharing early worksheets, the fun of reshaping, cutting, adding, the whole sport of revving up, of developing the poem. And the other loss--I am speaking of our professional relationship--was that she would not be there as we spread the poems for the next book out on the floor and tested what poems went with what others, what comprised a section, etc. The fun of format, if I may call it that, something we had always done for and with each other.

CD: You conclude your elegy for Anne, "How It Is" with this promise: "Dear friend you have excited crowds/ with your example. They swell/ like wine bags, straining at your seams./ I will be years gathering up our words,/ fishing out letters, snapshots, stains,/ leaning my ribs against this durable cloth/ to put on the dumb blue blazer of your death." Thirty four years after Anne's death, do you feel you've carried Anne's mantle, worn her "blazer," while maintaining your own distinct voice?

MK: I certainly feel I've maintained my own voice. "The dumb blue blazer" that I carry is, I think, common to anyone who has lost a dear friend to suicide. I've written several elegies to Anne, some addressed directly to her, as in "How It Is" and "Splitting Wood at Six Above," others in the third person. I hope that with "The Revisionist Dream" in *Still To Mow* I'm finally shriven. I say that with more confidence than I feel.

CD: This is humbling to hear and gives me a clearer idea of one of your more abiding muses. With regard to some of your other influences, I see strong influences of Auden in your work.

MK: Well, Auden absolutely, I'm happy to own up to Auden.

CD: How about Elizabeth Bishop?

MK: I don't think I was influenced at all by Bishop. I hardly read her at that time.

CD: You're often compared to Bishop.

MK: But it's true I had hardly read her. We sat next to each other once at a dinner in Harvard's Leverett House and she showed me pictures of her pet goats. I was too shy to utter a word about poetry so we just talked about animals.

CD: But there's a similar perspicacity, clarity, and accomplished formalism in your work.

MK: Well, it's possible that we may have shared some the same impulses, but I don't think so.

CD: How about Robert Frost and John Holmes?

MK: Well, John Holmes of course was my Christian academic daddy, he conducted the first workshop I ever took part in, and he got me my first ever job, teaching freshman comp part time at Tufts. There were two men who were very helpful to me. One of them was my tutor at Harvard, Harry Levin, who interceded for me after I flunked the Latin exam required for my Master's. At that time you had to write out translations from one modern and one ancient language. The French was easy, and I thought I would ace the Latin, on the basis of my top grades in high school, but I didn't. Levin stepped in and said, "Since it's obvious this candidate is not going on to pursue studies for her PhD. at this time"-I was eight months pregnant-"I vote we grant her the degree." And they did. So the master's degree was my ticket to my first teaching job.

CD: That was equivalent to an MFA in those days.

MK: Well, there was only Iowa's MFA program at that time. And because I was a woman I was only allowed to teach the phys-ed majors and the dental technicians. John Holmes, who was a professor in the English Department there, was a major influence on my emerging self as poet. He took Anne and me to New York to a meeting of the then-nascent Poetry Society of America.. He took us over to Harpers Magazine to meet Bob Silvers, who was the poetry editor. I credit him with really boosting me in as many ways as he could and giving me a visibility that probably helped me to break into some of those major publications. Garnering these credits for the acknowledgments page, of course, made publishing a book that much easier. And then I should say there were several other men who helped me along. There was Dudley Fitts, who judged the Yale Younger Poets Prize that year and awarded it to George Starbuck for *Bone Thoughts*, a brilliant book, and declared Sylvia and me tied for second place. He found us each a publisher.

CD: Did you know her at all?

MK: I knew her, but we were only acquainted. It was the year that she and Ted were in Boston and came to meetings of the New England Poetry Club and showed up at various readings around town. We used to call him Ted Huge because he was so tall.

CD: Actually, Sylvia refers to him in that way several times in her journal.

MK: But anyway, Dudley Fitts found me an editor in Stanley Burnshaw at what was then Holt, Rinehart and Winston and they published "Halfway." I think it was in an edition of 1,000 copies; of these I suspect they pulped 700. But it was a book.

CD: It was a book.

MK: It was such a thrilling moment.

CD: The poem "Halfway," the first poem in your first book of the same title. works as such an effective primer for the poems that follow, establishing your formal skill as a poet in writing about such taboo subjects--at least taboo for women--as madness, atheism, menstruation, incest, family tension etc.

MK: That was my extremely formal period, where virtually every line was metrically exact. Most of the lines end with exact rhymes. It was before I knew about how to use slant—approximate—rhyme and it was before I gave myself the freedom to write outside iambic pentameter or tetrameter.

CD: Right, but you were good at it. Not everybody's good at it.

MK: The rhyming, and especially the taut tetrameter line, I learned from studying Auden, I considered him my master. I have a little poem that's coming up in Prairie Schooner, titled "Symposium." It's a villanelle about going to hear Auden give a reading. He always wore his carpet slippers, an unselfconscious act I admired, so one of the refrain lines picks up on the carpet slippers. And you know Stephen Spender is reputed to have said of him, "Poor Auden, pretty soon we'll have to take his face off and iron it out to see who he is."

CD: Did you ever meet Auden?

MK: No, but I really worshipped the poetry. It was very meaningful to me.

CD: You have a similar dual inspiration, to be public one minute and private the next. That's particularly tough to pull off, to be able to speak as resonantly and poignantly in both modes.

MK: I've become more courageous as I've aged.

CD: I think you've been doing this all along.

MK: Well, I don't know about the courage part.

CD: Each of your books, from your first to your last, contains political poems.

MK: Yes, I guess so. “Heaven As Anus” is quite an early poem-I was attacked by Dinesh Di Souza for it.

CD: You were?

MK: I was indeed. He said it was a pornographic poem. Pornographic? He must have some extreme anal fixation or something.

CD: So Allen Ginsberg can write a poem called “Sphincter” but you can’t write a poem called “Heaven As Anus”.

MK: Right. I still like that poem.

CD: A religious object lesson.

MK: Well, a way of expressing my indignation at the way we abuse animals for our own gain.

CD: You turn a lot of Judeo-Christian theology on its head in that poem.

MK: I’ve done that to God a lot.

CD: What makes your poems interesting in that area is that they’re not two-dimensional announcements. You’ve got a quarrel going on, which is much more interesting. For instance, your Bread Loaf poem.

MK: Oh, "Young Nun at Bread Loaf"?

CD: If people didn't know about your background you would think this is a first encounter with a nun. But, of course, you were raised by nuns.

MK: But my nuns were in habit, severe black with white wimples, and they were sensational, in a way. They were regal, queen-like in a way that contemporary nuns in their drab mufti just don't rise to.

CD: No, no. But you're drinking your scotch, and she's drinking her tomato juice. And you're smoking a cigarette. But you're still picking mushrooms together.

MK: Chanterelles.

CD: That's refreshing. There's something going on there that is natural.

MK: Well, it's a narrative, and I believe so strongly in the place of narrative in poetry, including lyric poems. This is my big quarrel with students. Well, quarrel is an overstatement, but this issue comes up a lot in workshop. I just cannot get excited about a poem that has no narrative thread. It doesn't arouse my interest to the point where I am willing to, how shall I say it, invest in the language of the poem, language without meaning or emotion.

CD: I know Philip Levine loves your poems for this reason.

MK: Well, talk about narrative thread, you know? Levine rises to the top.

CD: You have both relied heavily on narrative. Have you been influenced at all by Levine's work throughout your career?

MK: I certainly have enjoyed reading his poems. I'm never bored by a Phil Levine poem. I admire what he does. He's a very angry fellow on the page. Off it, he's a sweet man.

CD: But it's that anger that is a vital source of energy, in both your work.

MK: Even in the poem I was just referring to in which the vet says, "We'll give her one more season on grass and then we'll put her down. Find a good place to dig the hole." And my rejection of that, because she looks terrific, my supposedly dying horse. I'm not putting her down. So there's a certain edge to my lines.

CD: Maybe the word you're searching for here to describe yourself is defiant.

MK: Okay, I think that fits. I'm defying death for her, and I'm actually defying death for myself. You can't live to this age without thinking about it, and how you're going to leave. And I then think back to Emily Dickinson's time when so much emphasis was put on how people die. Did they go calmly? It was important that the end be perceived as gentle. No "rage, rage against the dying of the light." I've chewed on this bone in "Death Etcetera," the last poem in *Still To Mow*.

CD: The last lines of the poem capture a profound pathos. "We try to live gracefully/ and at peace with our imagined deaths. But in truth we go forward/ stumbling, afraid of the dark,/ of the cold, and of the great overwhelming/ loneliness of being last."

MK: Well, here we are. Victor's going to be 87 next week. I'm 83. And, we're hanging on here. Fortunately, we have a good live-in caretaker.

CD: What is especially poignant about these lines is that notion of being last. No matter when you die, you're always the last in some respect. Of your generation, of your family...

MK: Yes, we're both orphaned, in a sense. I've lost three brothers.

CD: And you've written a beautiful elegy about your brother Peter called P.W..

MK: Yes, my brother Peter. Watching him die of ALS was possibly the hardest single thing in my life.

CD: I didn't know it was ALS.

MK: He was my closest sibling in age and we remained very close even after he had moved to California with his family. He was an engineer.

CD: Like Victor.

MK: Yes.

CD: What's so striking about this poem in particular is the incest section titled "The Incest Dream." The risk you take in writing such a dream is, again, courageous. Your language rises to the occasion with a haunted, Plath-like syntax, that is nonetheless all your own for the intense private emotion that emanates from your love for your brother.

MK: Did Sylvia have a sibling?

CD: Yes, a younger brother named Warren who became well known mathematician at Harvard. But, again, this poem has your own signature on it as a radical love poem that crosses traditional boundaries with a groundbreaking atavism that transcends sexual taboo. Its sisterly affection and grief are almost overwhelming. This poem scrapes the stone floor of the psyche in a way that's reminiscent of James Wright's elegy, "To the Muse." In both poems, the muse of grief appears to speak directly to the poet.

MK: Well, this is the role of poetry.

CD: I especially love the way you leap from your confession of love in the penultimate stanza to your dream of your brother' penis in the last stanza. Would you mind if I read these two stanzas to illustrate this point?

MK: Not at all.

CD: "Listen! I love you!/ I've always loved you!/ And so we totter and embrace/ surrounded in an all-night garage/ by theatergoers barking for their cars,/ the obedient machines spiraling down/ level by level as we block/ the exit saying our good-byes,/ you tangled in your cane, my black/ umbrella flapping like a torn bat.// At 3 a.m. I'm driven to such extremes/ that when the sorrowing hangman/ brings me your severed penis still/ tumescent from the scaffold/ yet dried and pressed as faithfully/ as a wildflower/ I put it away on my closet shelf/ and lie back down in my lucky shame." You are more purely lyrical here than usual. Of course, you are recounting a dream and dreams often have little regard for a coherent narrative. You have also written a lot about your children.

MK: It's true. I have used my family shamelessly.

CD: Shamelessly?

MK: I mean without holding back.

CD: The "Bones" poem, the "Soup" poem. You're full of wonderful contradictions in your work. One minute there's this tenderness, this wonderful loving tenderness, and then the next minute they're changelings.

MK: Yes, that's what happens when you have teenagers.

CD: But the way you write about them, there's an honesty and a closeness to the earth, with a literal attentiveness. Frost wrote in his poem "Revelation," "'Tis a pity if the case require/ (Or so we say) that in the end/ We speak the literal to inspire/ The understanding of a friend." In so many of your poems you speak the literal to a friend without worrying too much about being figurative, and it's working for you.

MK: I hope.

CD: Could talk a little about this? You said you were stubborn, and often you add that stubborn tension to what actually happened in your poems. Your essay and poem about Anne Sexton, "How it is"—it's so literal, so attentive to the way it was.

MK: Well I've written probably seven or eight elegies for Anne, about Anne, the last of them being "The Revisionist Dream" in *Still to Mow*.

CD: It's a villanelle.

MK: It's a villanelle. Well that's what I do. When a subject is too hot to handle I use the oven mitts of form.

CD: Form reflects the age often, or vice versa, but in looking back on your almost 60 years of writing and publishing, do you feel you've conformed too much or too little with the de rigueur of free verse that has largely prevailed as the dominant American form of choice since about 1960?

MK: I can't really speak to that because I don't really see what I'm doing while I'm doing it. I'm not writing as rigorously in form as I did early on, but I think I'm still writing in form for the pure love of it. There are two villanelles in *Still to Mow*. There are two dog sonnets, not quite pure. Also a pantoum. There is a sonnet, the last poem in *Jack*.

CD: But there's also the echo of form in most of your work.

MK: I love working with slant rhymes. I love hearing that echo in my head as I go along, and I love alternating long lines with short lines, which is what I seem to be doing in my most recent work.

CD: Yes, but that music, the rhyming, seems integral to both your breath and voice, wouldn't you say?

MK: Yes, I agree.

CD: It creates in your reader a sense of expectation. One wants to hear that skill or music you create in poems like "Morning Swim" or' "Sisyphus" or "Halfway." Or your sonnets "Purgatory" and "Prothalamion." You talk so subtly to yourself in form and rhyme--in an incantatory way, as you do in "Morning Swim" and "Sisyphus." I love the penultimate couplet in that poem: "One day I said I was a Jew./ I wished I had. I wanted to." You're overhearing yourself in these poems in such a hypnotic way that you lure your reader into your speaker's world or experience to the point of causing her to identify vicariously with your speaker's self-recriminations or confessions or epiphanies.

MK: Well thank you. What can I say to that?

CD: Am I right about this? Only you would know if you are talking to yourself in your poems.

MK: I haven't been conscious of it, but once you point it out of course I can see it. And, I think I'm still doing that.

CD: Your speaker becomes much larger than you. You create a kind of mythic self as a young and older woman who has broken out of the norms and strictures of cultural expectations and found an expression that transcends convention. You create a new way of thinking and talking, for women in particular, through thinking boldly about your most urgent human concerns as a woman.

MK: Well, I am a woman poet, and I have to write from that female point of view. I've always been a feminist, I feel in a way that it's my mission now to help young women writers when our paths cross.

CD: Some specific avenues you have opened for women include writing about your family and your past without censoring yourself, without at the same time shocking your reader for the mere sake of shocking him or her.

MK: Yes, but look at what Anne did. She broke all the taboos. I mean it's true. Ginsberg could write a poem called "Sphincter," but when she wrote her poem "In Celebration of My Uterus" or "The Abortion," she was savagely attacked. I think it's shocking to look back and see James Dickey, of all people, saying he didn't want to hear any more about her internal organs. He was offended. He, who went on to write *Deliverance* with its graphic scene of male rape.

CD: For women over the last 60 years personal or confessional poems have also worked as public poems in many ways. Some of the most famous that come immediately to mind are "Lady Lazarus," by Sylvia Plath, "Her Kind" by Anne Sexton, "Morning Swim," by you and "Diving Into the Wreck" by Adrienne Rich.

MK: You don't mention Denise Levertov.

CD: Yes, of course Denise Levertov.

MK: The funny thing is when Denise was writing all of those poems about the Vietnam War, I was disappointed. I thought she was going down the wrong track. I was afraid she would lose her lyricism in the process. And then of course, I've now done a similar thing in *Still to Mow*. So I understand much better. And Muriel Rukeyser too. I mean I secretly thought Muriel's poetry was too prosy even while I had great admiration for her courage as a war resister and a protester against dictators of any stripe. Now I read her appreciatively, empathetically. She was a remarkable woman.

CD: How about Marianne Moore?

MK: Marianne Moore was such a distant figure. The poetry certainly didn't move me when I first came to it. In truth, I don't value working in syllabics in English. Maybe in another language it would be meaningful, for example, in Russian, where the stresses are more obvious— but in slippery English I just don't see the point. I can see her work much more clearly, now. She was a miniaturist of the exotic. She was a real pixie.

CD: Very exotic.

MK: Oh, listen, you need to read the letters. In fact, I reviewed them for *The Women's Review of Books*, and that was a fascinating trip—such elaborate sycophancy. It's both revolting and wonderful to see how she cozied up to all those wealthy women with jewels and scarves who were always giving her presents. How incredibly sycophantic she was in her ever so carefully phrased thank-you notes.

CD: Just out of curiosity, you said you weren't influenced by Bishop at all, but did you read her?

MK: Oh yes, I do now. In fact I'm just reading a wonderful essay on her that's in the new *Hudson Review*.

CD: So you do enjoy her work.

MK: I like her very much. I think it's a pity she wrote so little.

CD: Yeah, it took her a long time.

MK: Well, it's one thing to be fastidious, but in a way it was a pity because there must have been a lot more poems stuck in there that never got out.

CD: I know often when I correspond with you, you say, "Well I'm going through the worst drought right now." You're worried about whether you'll ever write again.

MK: I think I caught that disease from Howard Nemerov. After every poem he would say dolefully, "Well, that's it, I'm done, I'll never get another one."

CD: But you've been so amazingly prolific.

MK: Well thank goodness, you know, I had a little breakthrough. I do have a long dry spell every winter. And now I've got maybe fourteen new poems over the last two years, so I'm happy about that.
CD: If we could for a moment return to the subject of your pastoral, private voice that's also public, I'd appreciate it since what you said earlier about the political ramifications of your private voice as a woman is very important and needs a little more clarification. I think it's perhaps been easier or more natural for women to find a nexus between their personal and political lives. This was especially true of Plath, Sexton, Rich, Levertov, and Rukeyser, to mention only a few again. I don't think men writing about their private lives have been

as conscious about such a nexus. There are exceptions of course. I'm thinking of Galway Kinnell's *Book of Nightmares*, W.D. Snodgrass's *Heart's Needle*, much of Robert Lowell's work following *Life Studies*, and Frank Bidart's *Sacrifice*.

MK: The difference is that it's still a brave new world for women. There's still so much to retrieve that has been denied.

CD: Do you see this dual role of the feminine voice continuing for some time, combining the domestic and political?

MK: You're always going to see a combination of the domestic and the political in poetry by women because they are assigned the domestic role by the culture. And, after all, biologically, we bear the children and we suckle them and then they go off to war.

CD: You were just saying that there are several black women writing now who are vital new voices, such poets as Rita Dove, Thylias Moss, Harriet Mullen, Toi Derricotte, Elizabeth Alexander, Lucille Clifton, Camille Dungy, Natasha Trethewey, Harryette Mullen and Patricia Smith.

MK: I think the poetry world has welcomed them.

CD: Yes, speaking of which, this big tent of American poetry, I'm wondering how you feel about it. I talked at the start about the crowded landscape of American poets, but didn't really follow up on this point. What do you think about the myriad voices that now appear in literary journals and books of poetry, compared, say, to your generation when it was starting out?

MK: From my vantage point I think the more the merrier. I've always felt that way. There's always going to be an awful lot of bad poetry written and bad poetry published, but I think eventually it gets winnowed out..

CD: So with all the stuff on the Web, along with the exponential growth of little magazines and MFA programs, who in the world is going to sort it all out?

MK: The next generation.

CD: That's who will worry about it, the next generation.

MK: If there is a next generation.

CD: I went to Associated Writing Program conference a couple years ago, not last year, and felt overwhelmed by its size.

MK: No, I don't go anymore.

CD: There are two many ballrooms of journal and program booths for me to take in. But perhaps this is just me.

MK: Well I stopped going about four years ago. I just can't.

CD: There's a movie called "Moscow on the Hudson" with Robin Williams. I don't know if you've ever seen it.

MK: Yes, I vaguely remember.

CD: It's early mid-80s. He plays a defector from the Soviet Union at that time. And he defects in Bloomingdale's– he was a clown in a visiting circus –he makes an American friend. He's hilarious. At one point in the movie, right after he defected, he's looking down Madison Avenue, Times Square and he sees all the lights and billboards and crowds of people. He turns to his American friend and asks, "But how are you supposed to know who the poets are?" There are hundreds of American poets, voices amidst the crowd, hiding in the open, but who's listening?

MK: I think we have to wait and see.

CD: Okay, well, one reason I think it's so important to interview poets of your generation is to see what you and your colleagues think about what's happening now in, as you also call your farm on Harriman Lane here in southern New Hampshire, "Pobiz." You're hopeful?

MK: Absolutely, I'm hopeful. I think it's so healthy to see this burgeoning. And as I said, ninety-nine percent of it may turn out to be trash, but that's not for us to say.

CD: That's helpful for me to hear, someone who's a few generations behind you.

MK: Let me just say I have a small window through which to view the present landscape. This summer I did a weeklong workshop at Provincetown and then I came back and I did three workshops at New England College and now I'm going up to the Frost Place to do a workshop, so in a small way I get to look at what the newest would-be poets are writing now.

CD: It's obviously both meaningful and important for you to write repeatedly about your garden, your animals and your neighbors. In a lot of your poems you place another before you. Whether it's the horse in "Jack," or the dead dog in "Apparition," or Stanley Kunitz in "For Stanley, Some Lines at Random," you are placing others before you. In doing so you create what Malcolm Cowley called the "transpersonal self." He used this term specifically in relation to Whitman's speaker. It's a self that crosses over from the speaker of the poem to the other placed before the speaker. This is what Bishop does in "The Waiting Room" when she equates her speaker, Elizabeth, with her Aunt Consuelo. This is what poets have done forever.

MK: For centuries. What fascinates me is, looking back, I remember a time when Whitman was not even in the canon.

CD: And Dickinson too.

MK: Dickinson too. And certainly Edna St. Vincent Millay.

CD: She was another one I wanted to ask you about.

MK: I knew so many of those sonnets by heart when I was fourteen.

CD: I can hear her in you. Are you aware of her influence?
MK: Not really, consciously. I mean the only influence I can truly point to is a dead white male, W.H. Auden, and I think I took his lines into myself by osmosis. God, those poems are just in me forever. "I sit in one of the dives on 57th street, uncertain and afraid." "Earth receive an honored guest." He was able to take this very conversational tone and write about contemporary events. And do it

metaphorically. “In the nightmare of the dark/ All the dogs of Europe bark.”

CD: In his poem “In Memory of W. B. Yeats,” Auden talks about Yeats being hurt into poetry. Do you remember that line?

MK: I do remember. “Mad Ireland hurt you into poetry.”

CD: How do you feel you were been hurt into poetry?

MK: Well, it’s probably more hurt by it than hurt into it.

CD: I think every poet who has written for as long as you is hurt into poetry.

MK: I think poetry for me was a major liberation. I was so shaken as a 17 year old freshman at Radcliffe when Wallace Stegner told me I should not try to write poetry, to say it with flowers instead. For years after that chastisement I didn’t write and then finally, about eight years later, I started up again. But I wrote in the closet until I heard about John Holmes’s poetry workshop at the Boston Center for Adult Education, and that was where it all began for me in 1957.

CD: Did Stegner just think you shouldn’t write because you were a woman?

MK: Who knows. Maybe unconsciously that was a factor. He was only four or five years older than I was, believe it or not.

CD: Stegner?

MK: Yeah, he was a brand-new instructor and I was a quivering 17 year-old freshman. I don't think it had much to do with gender. I mean I'm sure what I gave him was flowery and terrible, but they were actual rhyming sonnets and he told me to say it with flowers, not to write poems about it. The "it" being romantic yearning. So that was all I needed to hear.

CD: Well, in your poem "400 Meter Freestyle" you talk about picking up swimming first.

MK: Becoming a serious swimmer, that was my first bursting out of the cocoon of the family. In high school I swam for the women's amateur athletic team.

CD: Right, you were good.

MK: I was a good distance swimmer; I was not a good sprinter. I could never get off the block fast enough.

CD: At some point you must have said, "You know what? I can write. I can find the words. I can ride this wave out of here."

MK: In a way I suppose that's what happened. I rode that wave out of suburban Boston, out of that constricted life in the suburbs.

CD: Out of Brookline?

MK: Newton. We chose it because it had a great school system but everything else about it I detested. Once I was planted here in New Hampshire my whole world turned around.

CD: And not only did it turn you around, you seemed to find something you didn't know you had been looking for.

MK: No, I knew I had always been looking for horses. I had longed for a horse of my own from early childhood on. I never could have more than an hour a week on a hired school horse out of a livery stable. I was in my forties before I had my own horse.

CD: I think I hear the vet arriving. I feel we could go on talking about your work and life for many more hours.

MK: I know we could but we can't.

RUTH STONE

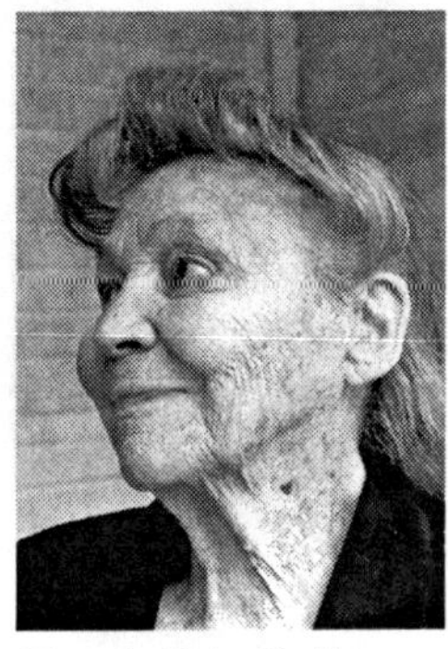

Photo by Najat Croll

This interview almost didn't happen. Although I had carefully arranged a date and time with Ruth Stone on the phone to meet, Ruth asked each time I called who I was and what this interview was for. I would later discover this was a ruse Ruth had devised to discourage me as an unknown visitor from meeting with her since her daughter and caretaker, Marcia Croll, was out of town, and she felt vulnerable as a 93 year old woman living alone. On the day of the interview, August 28th, 2008, I called Ruth on my way from home in Putney, Vermont to Middlebury to confirm our 10 o'clock interview. After more questioning, Ruth finally said she would meet me at noon, but she had to get dressed first. My wife, Liz, and I arrived at her address on Weybridge Street at noon and knocked on the front door of what appeared to be an abandoned house. No answer. We then walked around to the back of the house and knocked on a side porch door. Still no answer. I told Liz that I was going for a walk down the road for a while and that if Ruth didn't appear before I returned, I would abandon my plans to interview her. After a fifteen minute walk down Weybridge St., I returned to find an elderly lady and Liz sitting happily on the side porch in tattered lawn chairs. The woman was dressed in loose corduroy pants and a man's flannel shirt. Her long white hair, streaked with red, hung down to her waist and her brown eyes gazed out as if they saw everything and nothing at the same time. She smiled widely and deeply and laughed easily, emanating immediate affection, trust and vitality. She held Liz's hand, then rested her head on Liz's shoulder. I felt immediately that I was in the presence of a powerfully vatic woman. Liz said, "Chard, this is Ruth Stone." "It's an honor to meet you," I said. "I heard you knock but wasn't sure I should answer," she said. "Then I saw this beautiful red head sitting out here all alone on my porch and decided it must be all right." I sat down next to her and began talking and we didn't stop until three hours later.

CD: Do you think of music first before you write your poems? You often start your readings with songs.

RS: Well, you know, when I think back, I had a mother who sang all the time. She just sang old songs around the house.

CD: And you sang too?

RS: I was just used to hearing her singing, entertaining herself. And my dad had, well when he was a kid, his family let him go off one summer on a river boat where he was in the orchestra playing drums, my dad; that's what he was, a percussionist. Can you imagine? There I was with a mother who sang and a father who played percussion. What could I do?

CD: You write about sitting on your mother's knee listening to Tennyson, hearing poetry as well as her singing.

RS: It must have done something!

CD: And also your father's drumming, how could you not have become a poet?

RS: How could I escape?

CD: No way.

RS: Right.

CD: In your poem, "Where I Came From," you write that you were your own "quick woman." You also write, "My father put me in my mother/ but he didn't pick me out." I'm struck by your use of "quick," as well as your clear sense of independence as a person from the start. Was it your poetry that infused you with such a strong sense of independence and intellectual quickness?

RS: I'm trying to think, I'm thinking. Well, you know, I spent my childhood reading. I would lie on the bed on my tummy with a book under me and read. And I would read. I would read all night and my mother would get up and come in and turn the light out and as soon as she had gone back to bed, I would turn the light back on. And I'd keep on reading. I'd sometimes read all night long and then get up and go to school. I read in translation of course, the Russians, I was wild about them. Isn't that funny? I loved Dostoevsky, Tolstoy, everything.

CD: You have mentioned several times over the years that you aspired to write like no one else.

RS: That's right! I didn't want to sound like anyone else, so I wouldn't read any current poetry. I deliberately refused to read it.

CD: But you read a lot of fiction. In an autobiographical poem called "Pokeberries" you pay homage to your folk roots.

Pokeberries

I started out in the Virginia mountains
with my grandma's pansy bed
and my Aunt Maud's dandelion wine.

We lived on greens and backfat and biscuits.
My Aunt Maud scrubbed right through the linoleum.
My daddy was a northerner who played drums
and chewed tobacco and gambled.
He married my mama on the rebound.
Who would want an ignorant hill girl with red hair?
They took a Pullman up to Indianapolis
and someone stole my daddy's wallet.
My whole life has been stained with pokeberries.
No man seemed right for me. I was awkward
until I found a good wood burning stove.
There is no use asking what it means.
With my first piece of ready cash I bought my own
place in Vermont; kerosene lamps, dirt road.
I'm sticking here like a porcupine up a tree.
Like the one our neighbor shot. Its bone and skin
hung there for three years in the orchard.
No amount of knowledge can shake my grandma out of me;
or my Aunt Maud; or my mama, who didn't just bite an apple
with her big white teeth. She split it in two.

I'm intrigued by your embedded instruction, "There is no use asking what it means," in this poem. Would you mind indulging me a bit here by commenting on this line in light of the family history you provide in this poem.

RS: I remember saying it. Well, I think I would say it again. "There's no use asking what it means." But I'm saying it to myself. I don't know what it means. There's no use asking what it means.

CD: Can you say what you mean exactly by "it" in that line?

RS: I mean there's no use asking what any of it means. It's all true. You know, I never make anything up. I only tell the truth.

CD: What about your poem "Scheherazade"?

RS: I knew that story. Everyone knows the story of Scheherazade. I didn't mean I didn't fantasize at times. But what I talk about is true.

CD: So what you're saying is that you work from the literal, things that happened, actual experiences in your life…

RS: Right.

CD: But you often get very mystical about things.

RS: I think I feel mystical about them. I feel mystical about life, don't you? It's such an amazing thing.

CD: Although you credit your mother and your aunt with passing on that "splitting" strength to you, your father also seemed to instill you with a ribald spirit in the face of adversity.

RS: Yeah, I saw him that way once when I stopped in. I was on my way home from high school, you know, and I needed a dime to get home from downtown, and I went into the *Indianapolis Star*. He was working at the linotype machine. Poor dad, he worked all night on the linotype machine. There he was sitting in this swivel chair at this great big linotype machine and the lead was falling, And that was the first time I had ever seen anything there or seen anything about it. Now you know my father had never been very nice to me, my father was jealous of me, I didn't know this of course and he was critical. Oh God he was critical, and he called me sister you know because he had my brother back then, and he gambled too. When he got the paycheck he might come home, he might not. But we always, my brother, would leave the house and go all the way down to Washington St. and wait for him. Sometimes he'd come and sometimes he wouldn't, but when he came he would have candy and records to play on the phonograph. We had an old stand up, wind-up phonograph machine. It was just delightful, and he would read to us from the *King James Version of the Bible*. He would read Bill Nye. He would read all kinds of stuff. He finally came around once I got so much poetry published. He liked my poetry. My dad was all right, he was just nervous and critical and jealous of me, because I was the first child and my mother was just crazy about me, and my father got jealous. He worked at night and slept in the daytime too, you know, and we had a very small house, a bungalow, and he'd be asleep in bed in that room with the door shut and we'd have to be quiet.

CD: Despite growing up poor, female and self-educated, you somehow went on to become one of America's preeminent poets, winning the National Book Award, the Wallace Stevens Prize and just this month you were named as a finalists for the Pulitzer Prize for your book of new and selected poems, *What Love Comes To*. Yet, you have never seemed enthralled with the limelight, choosing to live and write as an outlier.

RS: I'll tell you why, because I'm a woman. That's why I'm in obscurity, at least one of the reasons. Guess who runs, the world, guess who runs the government, guess who runs everything. Men, darling men. And men only allow women what they want to allow them, and who wants to allow an old woman anything?

CD: But you should know that your poetry, your voice, your life force have transcended the male world that kept so many other women of your generation down.

RS: Thank you. Thank you. But you know, I've never thought of myself as a poet. Never.

CD: Because?

RS: I don't know why. I just never did. I never thought that, and not only that, I rarely read any poetry.

CD: Your mother read Tennyson to you as a child, and the *King James Bible*, and your poem "What You Need to Know Before You Join the Union" contains wonderfully satirical references to the pitfalls of the current "Pobiz."

RS: Well, yes, when I grew up I learned a few poems when I went to school.

CD: But your muse is so distinctly feminine, American, folk-like and literate.

RS: It's a funny thing. Even as a child, I would hear a poem coming toward me from way off in the universe. I wouldn't hear it. I would feel it, and it would come right toward me. If I didn't catch it, if I didn't run in the house and write it down, it would go right through me and back into the universe. So I'd never see it again. I'd never hear it again. I've lost about ninety nine percent of my poems this way. Sometimes I would catch the last line and write it through the bottom up. I have to say, I never thought they were mine. They weren't mine. They belonged somewhere else.

CD: So you feel like you were almost a conduit more than a self-conscious poet.

RS: Now that's not true of all of my work. Some of my work I have worked on and that's a matter of fact. Once when I was at Radcliff many years ago, they wanted me to give a talk about my work, and up until then I had thought that what I wrote was just instantaneous, and then I went back. I never throw anything away. I'm messy. I threw everything in boxes, so clothes and bills and everything else were mixed in with the poetry, but I found a poem of about fifteen, sixteen pages of revisions, revisions, work, work and changes, changes, changes. So I had worked on poems, not all of them. I remember one poem, "Things I Say To Myself While Hanging Laundry." I was out in the backyard hanging laundry, and the poem began coming to me and I went on hanging laundry, and all of a sudden I said to myself, "Oops, I better get this down." And so, I ran around to the front of the house, because I couldn't get through the back door because it was locked, and I ran up to my room, and started writing it down as fast as I could. I couldn't get the last line for years. I finally worked out the last line. But it's the darndest thing, because I wasn't focusing on what was happening, I was watching an ant cross on the clothesline, so the poem starts out with "an ant crossing on the clothesline/ from apple tree to apple tree,/ would think and think,/ it probably could not dream up Albert Einstein." I'm right back there in the back yard as if it were happening right now.

CD: The poem continues, "Or even his sloppy mustache;/ or the wrinkled skin bags under his eyes..."

RS (reciting): "…that puffed up years later,/ after he dreamed up that maddening relativity."

CD: "The ants cross its great fibrous forests,/ from clothespin to clothespin/ carrying the very heart of life in their sacs or mandibles,/ the very heart of the universe in their formic acid molecules."

RS: Now that poem just poured out of me, but it doesn't have anything but facts in it.

CD: Do you remember the last line that gave you so much trouble?

RS: "And there in the dark is Albert Einstein/ with his clever formula that looks like little mandibles/ digging tunnels into the earth/ and bringing it up, grain by grain,/ the crystals of sand exploding/ into white, hot radiant turbulence,/ smiling at you, his bushy smile,/ along an imaginary line from here to there."

CD: See, now there's your imagination. Those lines burned into you?

RS: I know everything. I never forget anything. Do you like that poem?

CD: I love this poem for its strangeness, its cosmic earthiness. You are a deceptively simple, as you say in your poem "All in Time." "I'm going towards something. I'm complicated, and yet how simple is my verse?"

RS: Don't you feel the same way?

CD: Yes, but to feel this way and to capture such extraordinary emotional range and oneiric richness are two different things.

RS: Well you know, what I'm trying to say is that for one thing, not very many people like poetry anymore I think. It used to be the troubadours, of course; they were the news carriers. But now we have the television and we don't need poetry. And popular music also has taken the place of poetry for many people.

CD: But you read good books, so then the question arises, why did you start writing poetry, instead of fiction or prose?

RS: I have written fiction, some of which I've published in such places as *Commentary*, and *The New Yorker*, and a lot I haven't published.

CD: Maybe you enjoyed writing poetry more.

RS: I didn't enjoy writing it more. The short stories came the same way, line by line. It was as if they were dictated to me. I've got notebooks full, but I don't think its any good, but I do it.

CD: Well you included ninety three new poems in your last book, *What Love Comes To*, the same number as your age.

RS: The thing of it is it's so interesting; it's like when I gave that talk. I thought I'd done it all the other way, but a lot of it I worked like crazy for. Now how do you account for my deluding myself like that?

CD: Perhaps your were so immersed in the writing process that the line between writing and revising became blurred.

RS: Maybe so. But I really believed it. I thought I hadn't done anything, and I had done all that work. Only on about half of them, half of them they came the other way.

CD: I'd like to turn to the subject of poverty for a moment since it plays such an important role as an idea and realty in your work and life.

RS: Okay.

CD: Poverty runs as a theme throughout your poetry as a spiritual paradox that yields great personal wealth and authentic lifestyle.

RS: Yeah, poverty. Well, what was I referring to, what time I wonder? "'I will,' said poverty."

CD: That is the final line in your poem "Bargain"—your answer to the poet's destiny as poverty's beloved, which contradicts the American dream of attaining wealth and fame.

RS: Well you know my father, as I say he gambled what money he made, he wanted to be a musician, but his father made him learn this trade of being a printer, he worked as a printer. And we lived in a two-bedroom bungalow, and momma gave me the other bedroom, she shouldn't have done it, and my brother slept on the couch in the dining room and that was it. And I mean that was it, we had a living room, two bedrooms, a bathroom and a kitchen and a little yard, and mother had flowers and so forth in the back yard, but I remember the spirea bush that was in the front yard. Also the porch was covered over, so we had a roof over it, so we had this little porch in the front yard. I remember on the Fourth of July, before he went off to work, wouldn't let us handle the fireworks and so forth, but at the end of the work day, we'd sit on the porch and he's shoot off firecrackers. He had blinded himself with fireworks when he was a kid, in one eye.

CD: You were about fifteen or so when the Depression hit, but even in your later life, you chose to live simply in a rural house in Vermont that had no running water or plumbing.

RS: I never thought about being rich or famous.

CD: In your books "Cheap" and "Second Hand Coat", you celebrate the richness of your domestic simplicity and closeness to the land.

RS: I had this… something about absolute something… I would never owe anyone anything, so I would never get anything unless I could pay for it right then, and I would never buy anything on time, so that limited me, of course, but that was the way it was.

CD: You don't seem to have missed it.

RS: No.

CD: You're not unhappy that you're not living in a big house in Middlebury?

RS: I've never really wanted things. I think people who want things are missing something. So things have to make up for it.

CD: Your line, "'Take me,' said poverty," is indicative of that.

RS: I used to come home from the library just loaded with books. I read through the children's library. I went to the high school library I went to the adult library. I read and read and read. That was my food.

CD: You have often been called a feminist for your strong themes of single motherhood, courageous widowhood, feminine witness to patriarchal injustices, and what you simply call "the female mind." But I think of you as a poet first, who writes about feminist themes and ideas, along with many other things. Do you feel I'm correct in thinking this way?

RS: I don't think I'm what you call a real feminist at all. I tried to be. I tried to be and I didn't know how. Because actually I had a brother I loved and I was not anti-male in any way. I loved men, you know.

CD: You write a lot about maternal subjects.

RS: Oh yes.

CD: That doesn't necessarily make you a feminist. Men and women alike are moved by your subjects and the way you handle them.

RS: Oh, that's a great compliment.

CD: You've written two poems that are particularly effective in this regard, "Being a Woman" and "Being Human."

RS: How do they go?

CD: Let's see, the one called "Being a Woman" starts, "You can talk to yourself all you want to."

RS: "You can talk to yourself all you want to."

CD: "After all, you are the only one who ever heard/ What you were saying, and even you forgot/ Those brilliant flashes seen from afar, like Toledo…"

CD: "Brooding, burning up from the Moorish scimitar."

RS and CD simultaneously, RS reciting, CD reading:

Sunk in umber, illuminated at the edges by fitful lightning.
You subside in the suburbs. Hidden in the shadow of hedges.
You urge your dog to lift his leg on the neighbor's shrubs.

Soldiers are approaching. They are everywhere.
Behind the lamp-post the dog sends unknown messages
to the unknown. A sensible union of the senses.
the disengaged ego making its own patterns.
The voice of the urine saying this has washed away my salt,
my minerals. My kidneys bless you, defy you, invite you
to come out and yip with me in the schizophrenic night.

CD: A remarkable poem. I especially admire the mythic voice in this poem that "yips" at the end in "the schizophrenic night."

RS: I'll tell you something. I went through a period when I became a feminist, but I gave it up. I gave it up and I'm not any longer a feminist. I discovered that among these feminists that I thought were so great they were not and they were unpleasant and selfish and icky just like everybody else. I'm for both sexes. There are wonderful men. Oh God, the world was created by men. I mean who's written all the gorgeous music in the world? Now I finally found out why men wrote all the music. I'll tell you why. Which of the birds sings the music? The male, not the female. The male is the wooer and he woos with his voice. He's the singer wooing the female and she comes to the beautiful music. But women are fabulous writers. They're storytellers. The grandmother told the story.

CD: You have those wonderful lines at the conclusion of your poem "Words." "A poet looks at the world/ the way a woman looks at a man."

RS: Well, she does.

CD: In your poem "Being Human" your speaker opines in an inclusive, philosophical voice while reiterating the same claim your speaker makes in "Being a Woman"— namely, that human expression amounts in the end to "meaningless eloquence."

We are still here where you left us
With our own kind: unstable strangers
Trembling in the sound waves of meaningless
Eloquence. They say we live.
They say, as they rise on the horizon
And come toward us dividing and dividing,
That we must save; that we must solve; transcend
Cohesive and repelling flesh, protoplasm, particles, and survive.
I do not doubt we will: I do not doubt all things are possible,
Even that wildest hope that we may meet beyond the grave.

RS: I'm speaking to Walter there.

CD: Although less gender specific in this poem, you make a similar point about the vanity of human eloquence, but then go on to embrace "the wildest hope" for the species ability to survive and even meet beyond the grave. But poetry seems to play no ultimate role in this survival and transcendence.

RS: What do you mean by poetry seems to play no role?

CD: When you say, "I do not doubt we will: I do not doubt all things are possible,/ Even the wildest hope that we may meet beyond the grave."

RS: Well I'm talking about my human love. That hasn't got anything to do with poetry.

CD: Earlier in the poem you say we're "trembling in the sound waves of meaningless eloquence."

RS: Just like we're doing now.

CD: But at least I'm trembling and enjoying our talk.

RS: Not all the talk about anything will alter anything, ultimately.

CD: So where does that leave poetry?

RS: You know the funny thing about poetry, and I'm sure you find it the same, is that the poems write themselves. You do know what you're doing but the poems just ... How do they do that?

CD: Well I was going to ask you that!

RS: Here's my theory. They're in the brain all right. Brains are so complex and they're just such a complicated thing. The brain talks to itself. I know it does.

CD: You've written a poem called "Connections" that discusses your "theory" of the cerebral process of perceiving and apprehending. It starts "What my eyes sees/ Goes into the dark/ And passes packet by packet/ Along the ledge over the abyss/ Between the lobes."

RS (reciting): "Between the lobes./ It goes so far/ I think I cannot get it back/ And when I least expect/ Some of it returns/ Not simple as it was/ Or seemed/ But now complex/ And freighted with the universe." I think that's really how it is. Our brains are so…well you know….They talk about us being the superior creature and all the time we underestimate birds and animals, my cat…my cat is very intelligent, very smart. We just underestimate everything.

CD: Which brings me to the continual presence of pathos in your poems. I am in awe of how effectively you confront grief in particular in much of your work. Many of your poems contain a remarkable mixture of grief and humor, sharpening your pathos to a razor's edge. I'm thinking of such poems as "The Moibus Strip of Grief," "Resonance," "Memoir," "Curtains," "The Talking Fish," "The Mold," "Loss," "Periphery," "The Room," all the poems in Who Is the Widow's Muse?, "A Love Like Ours," "The Womb," ""Against Loss," "Shadows," "Tenacity," "The Awakening," "For the Dead," "What It Comes To," "Memory," as well as several others.

RS: Well, you know how it is. Everybody loses what they love ultimately anyway. But, yes, it's rough.

CD: I would like to read a passage to you from Herbert Mason's translation of the *Epic of Gilgamesh* on the subject of loss and then hear your response.

All that is left to one who grieves
is convalescence. No change of heart or spiritual
conversion, for the heart has changed
and the soul has converted
to a thing that sees
how much it cost to lose a friend it loved.
It has grown past conversion to a world
few enter without tasting loss
in which one spends a long time waiting
for something to move one to proceed.
It is that inner atmosphere that has
an unfamiliar gravity or none at all
where words are flung out into the air but stay
motionless without an answer,
hovering about one's lips
or arguing back to haunt the memory
with what one failed to say,
until one learns acceptance of the silence
amidst the new debris,
or turns again to grief
as the only source of privacy
alone with someone loved.
It could go on this way for years and years
and has for centuries,
for being human holds a special grief

of privacy within the universe
that yearns and waits to be retouched
by something that can take away
the memory of death.

RS: Isn't that fabulous? I mean, he says it all right there. There is no need to say any more! Oh, who could say more? And yet, we keep going on and saying it over and over. And I don't know that work. You know, I don't know what you just read. And yet how do I know it?

CD: You do know it. The same duende or deep longing that infuses these lines resonates also from so many of your poems.

RS: It's built into us.

CD: Has writing poetry, in any way, retouched you with something that can take away the memory of death?

RS: I think that writing turns it over and over and over. Looks at it.

CD: The word "touch" recurs a lot in your poems about grief, along with the word "room."

RS: Room?

CD: Yes, both as a subject and place.

RS: Oh yeah.

CD: Such as the rented room you write about in "Against Loss."

RS: Oh God, yes.

CD: This a figurative place as much as a literal place for you.

RS: Yes.

CD: You make a courageous, ironic claim near the end of this poem, claiming that "Memory becomes the exercise against loss." You write about that room with a lot of courage.

RS: Yeah, it's weird isn't it? I guess, I never thought of it as courage.

CD: Well, probably it's good you didn't.

RS: You're probably right. I guess it is courage.

CD: Why do you feel memory serves as "an exercise against loss" instead of a grievous reminder of it?

RS: Because memory makes you relive it. You relive the living thing. So it isn't lost. You're re-experiencing it.

CD: Does that also happen in the writing?

RS: Something funny, I can tell you, is that when I'm writing I'm not experiencing anything. It's funny. The writing is separate. That's odd, isn't it? I don't write out of the memory of experiencing a memory. The writing is separate.

CD: Disinterested?

RS: I don't know whether I mean disinterested. It's separate from experience.

CD: But you're recalling the experience at the same time.

RS: I know. I know. Isn't that odd. It's like two separate things.

CD: Where are you then when you're writing?

RS: I don't know. I

CD: Yeats called it "the cold eye."

RS: That's a good description. It's just separate from everything else. There's no pleasure in the writing. It's like it's dictated to me.

CD: When you go back and read it after you've finished writing it...

RS: Then I remember everything connected to it.

CD: These poems are written from experience, everything's true in them, and you go right back to every detail, and yet when you're writing about those details.

RS: The words are completely separate from all that. Very weird. It's a weird brain thing.

CD: You have a generous muse.

RS (laughing): I'm just this weird old lady.

CD: Your humor complements your grief in a way that helps you write about loss without becoming morose.

RS: Yes! Ultimately, you know you can't help it. Life turns terrible, and it's so ridiculous, it's just funny.

CD: Your poem "Curtains" contains heroic humor in the face of one of your great struggles as a single mother, reflecting both your cageyness and toughness.

RS: How does that go?

CD: "Putting up new curtains…"

RS: Oh, yeah, "other windows intrude…"

CD: "as though it was the first winter in Cambridge…"

RS (continuing to recite):

when you and I had just moved in.
Now, cold borscht alone in a bare kitchen."
What does that mean if I say this years later?
Listen! last night,
I'm on a crying jag
with my landlord, Mr. Tempesta,
I sneaked in two cats.
He screamed, 'No pets! No pets!'
I become my Aunt Virginia,
proud but weak in the head.
I remember Anna Magnani.

I throw a few books, I shout.
He wipes his eyes and opens his hands.
OK OK keep the dirty animals
but no nails in the walls.
We cry together.
I'm so nervous, he says.

I want to dig you up and say, look,
it's like the time, remember,
when I ran into our living room naked
to get rid of that fire inspector.

You see what you miss by being dead.

You know, living with that guy was the strangest experience. Because he was this ridiculous man. The landlord. There was a fireplace in that apartment and he wouldn't let me use it. Even as I was living my life, I was aware that it was strange. Stranger than fiction. All of it. So peculiar. And how I got myself into such messes, I don't know.

CD: Well, it sounds like you got out of most of your predicaments.

RS: I would, I did. But I don't know how, how do we…are you in control of what you do?

CD: Not all the time.

RS: I don't think I am. I'm not so sure.

CD: Well, you're still here!

RS: I know but I seem to have…I don't know. I drifted into the darnedest situations. I don't know how. I think it was because I was alone.

CD: You traveled a lot throughout the course of your career as a teacher.

RS: I traveled and I had to get jobs and so forth.

CD: You moved to Vermont in 1957 after you won the Kenyon award.

RS: How did I happen to get that? John Crow Ransom was very nice.

CD: He gave you that.

RS: He gave it to me, yeah.

CD: And you also won the poetry award that same year, The Bess Hokin Award, right?

RS: Bess Hokin. Yeah, I don't know how that happened either. I think it was for poems in *Poetry Magazine.*

CD: Anyway, there must have been a little money that came along with that.

RS: Not much

CD: But you were able to buy the house in Goshen?

RS: It was very cheap then.

CD: You started coming up here and writing, and you stayed here.

RS: Yeah, you're right. Let me see how that happened. Was Walter dead? He died in 1959. I couldn't keep him from doing it. You know, he smoked and I think that he must have had some throat cancer and felt it and it was driving him crazy. I think that when he killed himself. It was for several reasons but you know, he was a heavy smoker. I had secondary smoke for years.

CD: You found something about living in Vermont inspiring and healthy. Was it the quiet and remoteness, along with the Green Mountains that reminded you of Virginia?

RS: The Green Mountains reminded me of the Blue Ridge Mountains, and also the silence.

CD: You're often quite wild in your poems, like the landscape in which you've lived. You seem so comfortable living and writing in your own "wildness."

RS: I'm crazy I guess.

CD: I would say sane.

RS: Yeah, I am, I am.

CD: But cagey enough to say in your poem called "Poems," "And you will take me in/ to your fractal meaningless/ babble; the quick of my mouth,/ the madness of my tongue."

RS: Do you know the funny thing about writing poetry is that you know what you're saying and you don't know what you're saying.

CD: Frost always said it was important not to know too much. But there's a sense of knowing a whole lot in your poems, but never more than the mystery you leave your reader with.

RS: Isn't that weird?

CD: In addition to writing so generously and prolifically about motherhood and your daughters, you've also written about your widowhood. In fact, you wrote a whole book called Who Is the Widow's Muse? They are both comical and sad poems. You titled them by numbers. I'd like to read Number 42.

After thirty years
the widow gets smug.
"Well I did it,"
she brags,
"with my own bear hands."
The muse shrugs.
"Uh-huh..
Did what?
The muse leads her to
a back stairway.
There is his undershirt
and his old trunk.
Smell that, the muse says.
The widow inhales his lost perspiration.
"You brute," she whispers.
The muse takes a bone

out of her arm
and knocks the widow senseless.
"She'll never learn,"
the muse simpers.

RS: Well, that whole thing…how did that start? I don't know, it just sort of…It's so weird how it just unwound.

CD: You haven't written another series quite like that.

RS: Well you know why? Leslie Fiedler said to me when I turned fifty…whatever it was, fifty two. He said fifty is the magic number, stop there. And so I stopped. And he said later that he regretted it.

CD: Your first chilling poem in that series betrays the perspicacity of your "cold eye."

Crow, are you the widow's muse?
You wear the weeds.
Her answer, a caw. Her black beads:
two jet eyes.
A stick fire
and a thorn for her body.
Into the wind her black shawl."

RS: Oh, those days.

CD: We talked a little earlier about your courage to face the subject matter that you face in your poems. The sorrow, the grief, and of course your ability to write about joy as well. But your courage simply to keep writing when you weren't publishing that much.

RS: You want to know, in my house, right now even here, I have metal cabinets with notebooks of poems. I've got so much, tons and tons of poems that have never even been transcribed properly on the page.

CD: What a trove!

RS: There are tons.

CD: In thinking about both the quantity and long trajectory of or your work, I find it interesting that you haven't written much about religious topics. There is one poem, however, from your book *Cheap*, that is rife with religious imagery. It is called "The Tree."

RS: How does it start?

CD: "I was a child when you married me."

RS: Oh, yeah.

CD: "A child I was when I married you./ But I was a regular mid-west child,/ and you were a Jew."

RS: That's right. Walter, my husband, was a Jew.

CD: But the Christ imagery here is strong and the formal music resonant.

RS: Yeah, it does show up doesn't it? Well, I think I get that from hearing my mother read the *King James Bible* to me as a child.

CD: "Love and touch and unity."

RS: "Parting and joining; the trinity."

CD: "Was flesh, the mind, and the will to be"

RS:

The world grew through me like a tree.
Flesh was the citadel, but Rome
Was right as rain. From my humble home
I walked to the scaffold of pain, and the dome
Of heaven wept for her sensual son
Who the Romans slew.

It was I who was old when you died, my Jew.
I shuffled and snuffled and whined for you,
And the child climbed up where the dead tree grew
and slowly died while she wept for you.

Well, what religion are you?

CD: I'm a backsliding Presbyterian.

RS: So was my father's family. I was raised in the Presbyterian Church. I remember when I was a kid being in Sunday school and hearing what they were saying and do you know what I said to myself suddenly. I was listening and I was thinking, I said this is not true. This is not true and I don't believe it, you know. From then on I had no religion. I could see easily enough that everyone came to death and was put in the ground. I think people have to believe. They can't stand it not to. How do you feel about it? They have to believe the other. I don't blame people for all of it, because they need that.

They need to have it. They can't stand the other. The fat that I stand it…I don't know what's wrong with me.

CD: But in your poem "On Being Human" you wrote about your wildest hope…

RS: Yeah. "Even that wildest hope that we"—Walter and I "—"may meet beyond the grave."

CD: But that's not a religious hope, as you say.

RS: No. I don't have any hope. He's a pile of bones.

CD: It's interesting you say that.

RS: Well, it's part of the poem, "that wildest hope." I mean I'm even saying "that wildest hope." Of course, there isn't any. I don't have any hope of it. None at all. No way. You get what you get when you get it. That's it. What do you think?

CD: I'm still trying to figure it out. I went to divinity school for three years and didn't grow any smarter about this. Where did you go to school?

RS: I hardly went to school at all. It's so weird. Why didn't I go to school? Well, my parents didn't have any money to send me to school. We were poor. So I didn't. I just read read read, and then when I had to go get a job, they just filled in that I had a degree and so forth for me, I don't have anything at all. I'm nothing.

CD: Did you go to high school?

RS: Yeah, I went to high school.

CD: So you're primarily self-taught.

RS: Well how do any of us learn? We learn by reading. I spent my life reading, so I'm educated whether I want to be or not. Of course going to college doesn't do anything for you.

CD: You've written about that in your poem "All in Time," which I'm still trying to figure out. These lines are very indicative of what you just said.

This language given me from birth
was not my language.
But in you, I knew a generous woman's voice.
You were puzzled, as I,
at the choices of death,
that we die at birth,
that we die as we are born,
denying ourselves and women.
Even you,
though you secretly gave me one eye which saw,
and one ear which heard.

RS: Yeah, my mom. I think it was my mother, wasn't it?

CD: What are you looking forward to now? Are you still writing?

RS: Yeah.

CD: Wonderful.

RS: I miss using a typewriter.

CD: But you're able to write by hand still.

RS: Yeah.

CD: And then someone types it up for you?

RS: No they don't, nobody does anything with it.

CD: Well how are you getting your work out?

RS: Nothing's happening. Nobody pays any attention.

CD: But you are the State Poet!

RS: Yeah, that doesn't mean anything. You know the governor, James Douglas, was awfully cute at the ceremony in Montpelier when I was installed as State Poet.

CD: He was?

RS: And he was sweet to me. Republican of course, and votes the wrong way. But you know…I think he's a decent man, but he is a Republican, I mean what can we do? What are we going to do?

CD: Do you still feel like you have a lot of poems inside you?

RS: I've got so much.

CD: And yet, you're resigned to being "swept away," as you write in your recent poem “Tell Me.”

RS: Oh, this is so revealing to me! How doe it go?

CD: It starts, “Ruth, how is your vision?”

RS (reciting):

“Lord,” I say, “know you not how it is with me?”
You who are blind to the sorrows of all things temporal.
You who are not even the wind sliding under the door;
how is it that I hear this echo?
catching even in my blind eye the death throws of a distant star?”
And you say, voiceless, as the forest of the mountains,
of the Sahara, of the Gobi, of the Kalahari.
Oom, ah, swept away.”

That’s one of my best poems. God, what the thing of it is I say to myself, how many sperm didn’t make it. Only one. And how the whole thing didn’t make it, but I made it. Amazing. The egg took in the sperm, the poor thing and it yelled and screamed and it didn’t want…That “Sperm and the Egg” poem is a good one. I’d been lying on the floor of my apartment. I don’t where I was, teaching somewhere. I had been really sick and I came to and that poem came out of me.

CD: Which one?

RS: “The Sperm and the Egg.”

CD: All of these special deliveries from across the universe.

RS: That's right. Special deliveries.

CD: So the fact that you're here as one among the billions who made it…

RS: Yeah, one among the billions. Amazing.

CD: You're reminded of the stars, right? Which is maybe why you love the galaxies and the universe so much.

RS: Weren't you amazed when you read that about that newly discovered star? That there's another one like ours, and I thought, Oh my gosh, probably there's other life out there now!

CD: So the fact that you made it and are aware and touched by something that has caused you to write poetry continues to amaze you?

RS: Oh my God.

CD: And not only made it, but survived to the age of ninety three with enough energy and inspiration to keep writing.

RS: I've survived because I have wonderful kids. My daughters are so kind and good to me I've survived partly because they've been good to me.

CD: Yes, and also your life force?

RS: How could I do it alone? How could any of us do it alone? We can't. Good heavens. What's the last poem in the book? I like that poem.

CD: “The Cave.”

RS: Read it to me.

CD: “The Cave”

My mahjong eyes weep
when the sky weeps,
when color fades
but it is the alphabet,
neat, succulent,

fresh slants of light
on the cave walls.
Oh skull. Your hieroglyphs
shine far down
the passage,
as if the vapors
wrapped around
this spinning rock
were sweet as lemon peel.

CD: This illuminated cave that is your “skull” and oracle rife with hieroglyphs and sweet vapors has transmitted a double message to you throughout your long career, a message that is both ecstatic and sorrowful, both hopeful and realistic, both finite and infinite. Nowhere is this more evident than in your poem “Train Ride.”

Release, release;
between cold death and the fever.
send what you will, I will listen.
All things come to an end.
No, they go on forever."

RS: They do.

DONALD HALL

This interview took place during the afternoon of January 9th, 2009, at Donald Hall's family farmhouse near Eagle Pond in Wilmot, New Hampshire. I began the interview by remarking to Hall that he was seven years older than Ezra Pound was when he interviewed him in 1960 in Rome for *Paris Review*. Hall appeared bemused and asked me to read his opening question, which pertained directly to the arc of Mr. Hall's own career. Hall asked Pound, "What do you think is the greatest quality a poet can have? Is it formal? Or is it a quality of thinking?" Hall then asked me to read Pound's reply. "I don't know," Pound had responded, "that you can put the needed qualities in hierarchic order. But he must have a continuous curiosity, which of course does not make him a writer. The transit from the reception of stimuli to the recording to the correlation, that is what takes the whole energy of a lifetime."

"Do you still agree with this answer?" I asked. Hall said, "For me, I think the sound that a poem makes has been my entryway to a poem, and Pound's ear was just incredible." Although I was already familiar with this *Paris Review* interview, I grasped the charge and intimacy of Pound's poetic transmission to the then thirty-two year old Mr. Hall. In that moment, my academic appreciation of Pound's responses to Hall's questions was transformed by Hall into very present "news" that transcended the fifty years intervening.

I then recounted Hall's confronting of Pound about his anti-Semitic broadcasts during World War II in Rome. Hall responded, "He was playing the tape when we got to that, claiming it was his Constitutional right and duty. But he didn't say anything conceptually irrational or crazy. He was your crazy Uncle Charlie, but he wasn't schizophrenic. He did say a couple of things that I didn't mention and I don't think I've said this to anybody. Maybe I did. We had lunch with Blair Fuller and his wife and Pound told a funny story. It was about a Catholic priest, a minister, and a rabbi in a pub. It wasn't making fun of the rabbi, but suddenly Pound's face went down. He said sadly, 'How did we get on the subject of race?'"

We talked further about this famous interview, but it soon became apparent that we were covering ground that Hall had already chronicled thoroughly in his essay on Pound in his book *Their Ancient Glittering Eyes*, so I asked Hall to discuss his poetic awakening. This question spawned a conversation that lasted for the next two and a half hours. I grew increasingly amazed by Hall's memory for both the details of his life events and brilliant language, particularly the precise syntax of quotes and lines of poetry, betraying a genius for grammatical accuracy, colloquial eloquence, and bittersweet wit. In his soft but intense, gravelly voice, I felt he was speaking to me from a vantage point that was both close up and far off—close up in his vivid recollection of events and far off in his well-seasoned hindsight sharpened by grief and writing.

As late afternoon came on, I sensed that our conversation had run its natural course for this particular afternoon. But it wasn't I who ended our exchange. As we were talking about his and Jane Kenyon's writing habits, Mr. Hall abruptly said, "Come here. I want to show you something." He then led me into his book-lined study. He proceeded to pull a few photo albums from a shelf and open them to pictures of Jane. I saw how thinly sealed over his grief still was and how important he felt it was for me actually to see various images of Jane—what he called her randy look in one and her spiritual visage in another—in the way he liked to remember her.

CD: Who were the first poets you read in your youth and how specifically did they influence your own development as a poet?

DH: My first poet was Edgar Allen Poe, who was a terrible poet. I liked him at twelve; I don't follow him now. Then I found Wallace Stevens, who I needed at the time—his development and coherence of sound, within either metric or free verse. Diphthongs repeated, or long vowels, some consonantal repetition, not so important as assonance or half-assonance. A diphthong is two vowels squeezed together, and you can play on the diphthong, one half of the vowel with another. "I" is ah followed by eee. The occasion of the poem is its sound. The start of the poem is often a mystery. Sometimes it's not. I have known most of my life that there is poetry for me in some landscape or some incident. Poems often begin with a given. I many times followed a given without having any notion of what it might mean then. It's necessary for me, not for everybody, to write a poem over and over again for a long period until finally I know what I'm talking about. On occasion, after I've reached a satisfactory resolution, somebody else has told me what I'm writing about. There's less conscious thinking in a poem than in prose. Less effort to make or reach a point or an argument, but a desire to make an aesthetic whole, primarily composed of resolutions of sound.

CD: You have written also about Ezra Pound's aural gift in your essay on him in *Those Ancient Glittering Eyes*, praising his ear for its uncanny manipulation of diphthongs and long syllables in his patented undulation of spondees and iambs. Did you find his influence, both his prosody and poetic ambition, a strong influence on your own work, particularly in your longest poem *The One Day*, which you wrote twenty years after you interviewed Pound for *The Paris Review*? Do you consider *The One Day* your *Cantos*?

DH: A very miniature version.

CD: You wrote that poem around the same time you wrote your essay “Poetry and Ambition.”

DH: Oh, whenever you read a poet’s essay, and you don’t know quite what he’s getting at, look at what he’s writing at the time. That essay was written as I was trying to write that poem.

CD: Were you thinking of the *Cantos* at all? As far as ambition?

DH: Not so much as European Modernism, not any work in particular. The abrupt changes, the juxtaposition by contrast. There’s an element of collage in that work. Later, in “Baseball,” I did find it. It’s really in “Praise for Death,” too, the juxtaposition of differing attitudes, ambitions, references, that are scattered but held together by a shape, ultimately attempting to be a single thing. I suppose that many of those words could apply to the early Eliot, not *Four Quartets* but “The Wasteland,” maybe “Ash Wednesday.”

CD: Do you feel those poems influenced you in any way in your early work?

DH: What you grow up with remains with you always. When I was fourteen I found Eliot. I bought a book I could still show you, which was called *Collected Poems*, but it just had the first texts. I bought it and I studied Eliot and I actually wrote comments in the margin, my words all misspelled. At the same time, I found Stevens, I found Cummings for a while and then got rid of him. Then Hart Crane was a big thing for me. His disjunctions are extraordinary.

CD: Much of your recent work emanates candid, recrudescent expression, as well as remarkable sprezzatura. The Italian Renaissance writer Castiglione, who coined this term, defined it in this way: "I have found quite a universal rule which in this matter seems to me valid above all other, and in all human affairs whether in word or deed: and that is to avoid affectation in every way possible as though it were some rough and dangerous reef; and (to pronounce a new word perhaps) to practice in all things a certain sprezzatura, so as to conceal all art and make whatever is done or said appear to be without effort and almost without any thought about it."

DH: You have to work hard to make it look easy.

CD: Yes. Could you talk a little about your own writing process?

DH: I often begin thinking I'm writing a single short poem, and find something new to add to it a month later. "Kicking the Leaves" was like that. I had no idea I was writing a long poem. Again and again in my work I have found a way to write and then it's gone stale on me. I have flailed about to find some way to write that allows me to speak again. When I find an alteration of style it begins as an alteration of sound. With "A Roof of Tiger Lilies" and subsequent poems, it was the short line with enjambed long vowels, often ending with a fantastic image. When that stopped working, way back in the sixties, one day I found myself writing the beginning of *Kicking the Leaves*. It opened things up. It was a long line from Whitman, but it was also asymmetrical, a long line paired with a short line. Various shapes. I had been writing tight poems, six or seven syllables per line, and I controlled the form by making each line discrete, musically discrete. The world became more and more obscure. With *Kicking the Leaves* I began to work by caesuras, rather than by short lines, and I felt an opening up of subject matter—the world—which seemed to originate in the sound of the lines. The subject matter didn't seem to come first. For a while then, I wrote rapidly. I would take a month to finish a poem, rather than a year and a half. These days I'm slow again. I just wrote one now that I like which I'm about to send out. It has 157 drafts.

CD: You counted them?

DH: I've taken to doing that. I want to brag about it! Now I feel I can move from one style to another, going past the things I learned and left behind me. And maybe I do not have the energy to write so much as I used to. Perhaps nobody has done his or her best work at eighty or after. Thomas Hardy was wonderful but nothing after eighty was among his best.

CD: I'm trying to think of an exception.

DH: Well, Walter Savage Landor wrote four lines in his eighties.

CD: The eighteenth-century poet who was famous for his epigrams. Do you remember which lines these were?

DH: "I strove with none, for none was worth my strife. / Nature I loved and, next to Nature, Art. / I warmed both hands before the fire of life; / It sinks, and I am ready to depart."

CD: I find your "Recent Poems" in your 2006 *White Apples and the Taste of Stone: Selected Poems* particularly bold.

DH: I hope you like my newer stuff. I had a terrible patch from 2005 into 2007. I became ill and three illnesses were the result of medication, two of them because of totally rare responses to a good medication, one a new bad medication. I spent two weeks in a nursing home at one point, and I stopped working on poems. I whistled in the dark, but I did nothing for another year. Then I knew I would never write again. After two and a half years I was depressed, then in the summer of 2007 I began to write again. I had stayed out of my study for a couple of years because it was so depressing, and on my desk there was a pile of folders, each including drafts of poems that went way back. Seeing those folders was horrifying. One day I decided to try reading them, and ran away. Then another day, I looked at two or three and fled. Then one day in a fit of bravery I went in there and looked through them all and threw away about half and kept all those that I saw something in. I had to throw half away in order to get to work again. I worked on older poems, several of which became unrecognizable compared to their drafts. It was that summer that I began the poem that took 157 drafts, that I'm about to send out.

CD: In 1975 you chose to give up your tenured academic career at the University of Michigan and move to Eagle Pond in Wilmot, New Hampshire to live and write with your wife, Jane Kenyon. How did you support yourself as a poet?

DH: By writing prose, as well as poems. I adored it. I would never have done it on my own. Jane was pushing me. Jane's family were freelancers in Michigan. They were musicians. When her voice went, her mother became a seamstress. They never knew what they would live on six weeks from now. My father had a conventional job all his life, and I had a regular job with tenure, cradle to the grave. Freelancing was terrifying. She really wanted to live here, which I did too, but how? We came here in August with the notion of camping out for a year. By October, Jane was saying that she would chain herself into the root cellar rather than go back. In December, I wrote a letter of resignation.

CD: They must have been shocked.

DH: The English department rejected it and gave me another year's leave without pay.

CD: Which must have made it hard for you?

DH: Not really. I had made a decision. Oh, I worried about money all the time. I did all sorts of things. There used to be a magazine called Ford Times, for people who bought Ford cars. I knew the guy in Ann Arbor who edited it. I read the biography of Gertrude Stein and
wrote a piece about her love for Ford cars. I got five hundred bucks! Needless to say I've never reprinted it.

CD: What an angle. So you continued freelancing in this way, suggesting your ideas to editors?

DH: I began by suggesting articles to magazine editors, and eventually editors were calling me up asking me to write something. Earlier, one thing that I had done in Ann Arbor was the draft of the textbook *Writing Well*. At the beginning that book sold a lot, and helped us get started here.

CD: And your book *To Read a Poem* must have done quite well also.

DH: And *Ox Cart Man*. After we'd been here for a year or so, my cousin Paul told me that story. "Have you ever heard the story about the fella that lived around here?" And I made it into a poem, which was in *The New Yorker*. Later I felt that the story could become a kid's book. I drafted the juvenile in about forty minutes.

CD: And that did well!

DH: It's still doing well! It won the Caldecott. It's a big seller in Japan and Korea.

CD: So looking back on that move now, what do you see that you have done that you never could have done if you stayed in Michigan?

DH: Oh I—there's just so much.

CD: Not just the writing, but the living.

DH: I'm an only child. I grew up lucky to be alone, not having many friends. I stayed in the house when my mother was away, daydreaming, playing a record over and over again. Then I went to Harvard, which is when my life began, and you know there were terrific poets there. Robert Bly, John Ashbery, Adrienne Rich, Frank O'Hara. Robert Creeley had just left. Maxine Kumin graduated the year before. It was incredible. I became social. I had friends. When I went to Ann Arbor I continued to go to cocktail parties. There were GM execs who lived in Ann Arbor because there was theater there. There would be three cocktail parties on Friday night and then five on Saturday night, but Jane really loved her solitude. When we came here, we had that; it was a solitude filled with work. Living together—I'm quoting myself—we had a double solitude. We'd get up in the morning and she'd walk the dog and I'd begin to get to work. She worked upstairs and I worked down.

CD: Right, you might as well have been in different states.

DH: About twice a year I'd knock on her door. Sometimes we met in the kitchen to have another cup of coffee, just slap ass and not even speak. Then we did speak, but people didn't come to our house for dinner parties, we didn't have them. Occasionally we'd have visitors from Ann Arbor or New York, but it was largely a solitude and silence that was so rich! I still have the solitude, but it's not double.

CD: But what you're saying is there was ironic company in that double solitude with Jane.

DH: Solace, but I wouldn't call it ironic.

CD: A silent but essential company.

DH: Absolutely. I knew she was here all the time and we loved each other. But we lived in a house with a great deal of silence.

CD: A house with many rooms.

DH: Yes. You talked about change in poetry—but oh, the change from that crowded social life! I lived with Jane in Ann Arbor for three years, and the summers we came here.

CD: She fell in love with this place.

DH: She was born in Ann Arbor but she loved this place, the house, the land, the little bit of the culture that she saw. Later she joined it thoroughly. Finally, people started to think that she was the New Hampshire cousin and I came along.

CD: You both found the solitude here invaluable to your writing and your lives together as writers.

DH: The simple solitude remains. Of course, one's energy diminishes with age. I work an hour a day on poems. When Jane died, I tried turning back to children's books, but I haven't been able to do it. I did a book of short stories after Jane died. I don't seem to have any prose energy now. I finished *Unpacking the Boxes* mostly before the two and a half year vacancy I spoke of. I was able to go back to it and make changes. There's not so much prose energy now. And, of course, less income. My income comes more from poetry readings than anything else.

CD: Well you did, up until Jane's death, have more prose energy than most poets.

DH: Robert Graves. I met him out in Ann Arbor. Did you ever read my story about him?

CD: Which one?

DH: It's a piece in Unpacking the Boxes. I told him that I envied him writing prose to support himself, to which he replied, "Have you ever tried?"

CD: Robert Bly has of course written a lot of prose.

DH: More translation. I'm not a fan of *Iron John*. I'm a fan of Robert Bly. We're still dear friends and we exchange letters, but we're terribly different. I remember when he told me he was writing Iron John, I said "Okay, don't send it to me." And he sent me the manuscript and told me to read it, and I read it and hated it. I wrote him and told him, and he wrote back saying, "I didn't sleep for four days." We've been like that with each other before, exaggerating. But he's working on poetry with great vigor right now and he's eighty-two.

CD: At a prose poetry conference several years ago in Walpole, New Hampshire, I recall Bly writing constantly in his notebook, then reading a new poem and asking, "What do you think?" Has he always done that?

DH: He'd say, "Oh, this is a poem I wrote this morning." I didn't know whether to believe him, but I like most of what he does. I'm the kind of reader who talks about words and he's the kind of reader who doesn't talk about words at all. He talks about analogies. He's the master of analogy. There was a time, back when we were in our thirties, I suppose, when we would actually rewrite each other's things. Simpson and I did that too. Liam Rector was the last one to do that for me. I need other people, not here, but by mail.

CD: In a letter to Robert Bly in August 1958, James Wright wrote:

The difference between what Dickey saw and said in Sewanee (Spring 1958) and what you saw and said, and what Simpson saw and said, and what Hall and Snodgrass have seen and done, is superficial. It is that we have learned the tricks too well, and that having arrived at a point of beginning, we have assumed that we were completed. All that happened to me is that I was stung awake, by Dickey who was cold and furious, and by you who were friendly and polite but equally uncompromising. Now, it may turn out that I do indeed have nothing in the way of vision and imagination. But I am stuck now; if I have nothing, I'm convinced that I can face the fact without bitterness; the new imagination is so important, to all living human beings and not just the literati, that I am going to continue to search for it—and if I cannot find it myself (though I believe I can), then I will identify and fight for it in others. And this is not mock-humility—I see blood in this matter, I really do.

Do you know what Wright means in this passage by "the new imagination" and being "completed?"

DH: Jim was given to totally sincere extravagances, of humility in particular. He wrote me lots of letters in which he renounced everything he had ever done. One thing he alludes to but doesn't speak of much is the quarrel about metric and non-metric. Bly at that time was violently against any meter at all. When we were undergraduates he was writing nifty iambic pentameter.

CD: Very formal.

DH: Very formal. "And I have seen the gulls of Bonaparte." He'd never seen the gulls of Bonaparte, he just liked the phrase. Smooth iambic. But on a Fulbright trip to Norway he read some European Modernists and Jim went to Austria and found Trakl. English-American Modernism was very different from continental. Bly had his Spaniards, and Jim helped him get to Trakl. Jim's German wasn't much. I think it was John Simon, in his review of Jim and Bob's translations, who wrote that it was an achievement to make fifteen mistakes in German, in one stanza. What they had been doing is going up to German farmers and saying, "Is this right?" And they would all say, "Yah, yah." They learned they had to go to German literary folks to check it. Bly has innate qualities of invention and analogy, not the ear, and he certainly loathed meter. Jim always loved metrics. And Jim would send me metrical poems and say, "Don't tell Robert." Jim was scared of Bob. I used to exchange poems with tons of people including Simpson and Bly, but it was useless to send one to Jim because he'd always say, "That's just wonderful." He did not want anybody to criticize his poems. If they did, he would say, "I am the worst poet in the world."

CD: Wright wrote many powerful raw poems. One of his poems about Jenny called "To the Muse" evokes such remarkable naked grief and desperation in particular. It actually reminds me of some of your later poems in Without where you bare your emotions unabashedly. You seem more interested in getting down the bare facts of Jane's illness, trusting your poetic instincts, than crafting these poems of extremity in any self-consciously poetic way. I think of the following lines from your poem "Without" where you alternate between lyrical reflection and anti-poetic medical language:

pain vomit neuropathy morphine nightmare
confusion the rack terror the vise
vincristine ara-c cytoxan vp-16
loss of memory loss of language losses
pneumocystis carinii pneumonia bactrim
foamless unmitigated sea without sea
delirium whipmarks of petechiae
multiple blisters of herpes zoster
and how are you doing today I'm doing

My poetry from *Without* to the present has been shedding its clothes.

CD: It's interesting you mention that image because you appear to enter into your own private bardo state. One of the main images for a bardo state is the shedding of clothes.

DH: There is a poem I was showing Linda [his companion] this morning. She said, "You will say things about yourself that nobody else would say." It was so far from what I was writing at the beginning. Just utterly so far. By the way, in my book of stories there are three about a character called David Bardo. This is mysterious. I was writing the first of those stories, trying again and again over a year or two, and I can't remember what the character was called, but when I named him David Bardo the story took off.

CD: It's a Tibetan word for transitional state.

DH: I knew it was Tibetan.

CD: In your poem "We've Come to Expect" you conclude with this observation about the Puritans: "…in Adam's fall and the broken promises / of the remnant--we discover ancestors / appropriate to our lapsarian state: / Their rage sustains us." Do you feel your ancestors' rage has sustained you?

DH: Entirely. I think.

CD: In the colorful voice of Horsecollar, who seems to be your version of John Berryman's Henry, you give yourself license to comment on subjects with the honesty of a Shakespearean fool.

DH: I see what you mean.

CD: You often write beyond the poem's conclusion in "Horsecollar's Odes", adding your own annotation on the poem you've just written. These annotations are often wise and humorous at the same time, each one beginning with the phrase, "Or say…" in the voice of Horsecollar.

DH: Who is also Citizen Zero. I hadn't thought of Henry.

CD: Who is your alter ego?

DH: Absolutely. Horace was my source and structure, but I wasn't translating his works at all. The connection to Horace was comedy. You know the poem, "When The Young Husband?" Horace's ode is about Achilles going to fight at Troy. On the way he stops at the island where Tiresias is, who correctly tells him that if he goes to Troy he will be killed. Achilles sails to Troy and gets killed. That was the ode of Horace's I was talking about.

CD: Horsecollar has the same irreverent, candid sensibility as Henry. Following your eloquent update of Horace's ode on Achilles, Horsecollar comments, adopting the style of his alternative Citizen Zero, which is, as you say, a "prophylactic smirking dog-cynicism": "Or say: Why this whining? You liked / your nookie well enough, / back when you had your teeth."

DH: Poetry is a device for saying something and taking it back at the same time. It's the device for double-mindedness or many-mindedness. No emotion is pure, but frequently we are aware of one and not the other. In poetry somehow you come out with both.

CD: In your poem “The Master” you write:

Where the poet stops, the poem
begins. The poem asks only
that the poet get out of the way.
The poem empties itself in order to fill itself up.
What may the poem choose,
best for the poet?
It will choose that the poet
not choose for himself.

DH: Do you know where I got that? Meister Eckhart. Meister Eckhart talking about God.

CD: I’m fascinated by your complex views on love in many of your poems. In your poem “Old Woman Whom I” you write:

It was love that grew eyeteeth, not for love bites:
it was love that made war, what other destroys
so thoroughly as love does? Revenge
and destruction are love’s two faces.

You follow up on this theme of love’s destructiveness in your poem “Gospel,”substituting hatred for love in a litany reminiscent of 1 Corinthians 13: “Hatred is wise beyond its years. / Hatred is intent, clever, and patient.”

DH: I began that poem after 9/11.

CD: Your poems on love display a Shakespearian suspension of emotional opposites.

DH: Conciseness and two-sidedness, as I say, are essential to poetry. Poetry exposes and explores more than any other art does, one of the great values of poetry. I began by saying I came to poetry for the sound it makes. The poem is a sensual body, or it doesn't exist. Did you ever read that interview that many of us did with Harper's? I was quoted saying that "poetry is oral sex." I wanted to get attention.

CD: Well, does it exist as some sort of ineffable music before it finds words? You were talking about meter before and your lifelong search for your own "meter-making argument," as Emerson would say, from the long narratives to the shorter lyrics. It's fascinating what you ended up doing with your early poem "Exile." You boil it down to six lines in your revision of it years later. That poem, at a very early stage in your career, presages so many of your later poems on death and dying.

DH: The six-line one?

CD: No, actually the longer first version. You leave out the prescient part in the six-line 1968 revision. This is from your formal 1953 version:

Exiled by years, by death no dream conceals.
By worlds that must remain unvisited.
And by the wounds that growing never heals.
We are as solitary as the dead,
Wanting to king it in that perfect land
We make and understand.
And in this world whose pattern is unmade,
Phases of splintered light and shapeless sand,
We shatter through our emotions and evade

Whatever hand might reach and touch our hand.
I hear Eliot in a lot of these lines. Your old subject matter of death and alienation are there, but you're not "yawping" yet. You make reference to "our emotions," but very little emotion actually emanates from these rather highbrow lines, unlike your more evocative but plain-speaking 1968 poem of the same title:

A boy who played and talked and read with me
Fell from a maple tree.
I loved her, but told her I did not.
And wept, and then forgot.
I walked the streets where I was born and grew.
And all the streets were new.

I don't know the precise date of your poem "We Explore Grief's Borders," but I find it equally prescient: "The coast is clear. Please come / out! This underground business has lasted too long: Relent. Relent. Relent. Relent."

DH: When Jane and I were together, every time someone close to us died we would go back to Henry King, "The Exequy." An incredible poem, that practically nobody seems to know.

CD: I especially love the last half of "The Exequy" where King directly addresses his young wife, wondering how to live on after her death. It's beautifully moving.

DH: Even though he believes absolutely that he will meet her in heaven, his expression ends in a coherence of grief. We would sit down and I would read it aloud to her, always.

CD: But here you seem so close to grief.

DH: My father died when I was twenty-seven. Wesley, my grandfather, died when I was twenty-three. He was seventy-seven. He was born in 1875. He died in March '53; he hadn't had his birthday yet. Elegy has been the center of my work all along.

CD: Your poem "Kicking the Leaves" also ends in a very Whitman-like way, reminding me especially of his repetition of the word death in "Out of the Cradle Endlessly Rocking." You write a similar litany at the end of your poem: "Now I leap and fall, exultant, recovering / from death, on account of death, in accord with the dead." Was there a time in your childhood when you became profoundly aware of death as a poetic subject? Or to put it another way, when you were deeply affected by someone's passing?

DH: There was a patch in my young life, early life, when I was about eight or nine when there were six deaths in my family in close succession. At eight or nine I said to myself, "Death has become a reality." That was my language at eight or nine, and I think that I was fixed on it, that early. My favorite novel, one I read over and over again when I was eleven or twelve, was called *Jimmy Sharswood*, and it was a novel by a poet called Roy Helton. Robert Frost loved Roy Helton; he wrote some beautiful poetry. *Jimmy Sharswood* was the boy in the book who died in the end. And I read it for the pleasure of the sadness.

CD: In your poem "Winter's Asperity Mollifies," you conclude, "Love / and death, love and death: how do you tell them apart?" And in your poem "Revisions" you have conjured this ordinary yet ecstatic ending: "In the bliss of routine, / —coffee, love, pond afternoons, poems— / we feel we live / forever, until we know we feel it."

DH: Yes, there were a couple of good things in *The Old Life*.

CD: How would you define "it" exactly in that last line, or do you feel what you're trying to describe there is ineffable—what Frost calls "the aftermark of almost too much love" in "To Earthward"?

DH: It's simpler than it seems, at least for me. If we know that we're feeling we're going to live forever, we immediately know it's not true. There is a long period of middle age where if no one close to you dies you live as if you were going to live forever, as if there were no such thing as death. It's curious at seventy to realize that at twenty, thirty, forty, fifty I would think "Ten years from now . . .". You can't think that anymore.

CD: I think that begins even sooner. I think it begins in your fifties a little bit, the taste of it.

DH: Well, my fifties were my best decade because I moved here with Jane and *Kicking the Leaves* came out. Most everybody reviewing my work has said that's where I really began. I moved in here just before I turned forty-nine, with Jane. So my fifties were a glorious time, and I don't think I felt the shortening of the future yet. My life started over again. I had a young wife, a poet who was at that point totally unknown and writing mostly inferior stuff, but just gradually, bit by bit, she became so good. It was incredible.

CD: You had no way of knowing she was going to develop into such a strong poet.

DH: I didn't know. She was my student in a class, where she was not the best. Other books came out of that class. Such as David Tucker's. He's had just one book. He was a newspaper man, working an eighteen hour day, trying to get up early and work on poems, and he finally did it and won that prize Houghton Mifflin gives out. There was another who published four or five books I don't think were so good. It was a terrific class. They said to each other, "You're full of shit." None of this patting on the back stuff. That's where I got to know Jane and like her. She wasn't very attractive at that time. She wore her hair short and straight, with thick glasses. She was nearsighted and she had acne. She always had a gorgeous figure. And there was something else. There was something about her rogueishness, not just sexiness. Everyone was being sexy around that time. And she was living with a guy, the only guy she ever lived with, and they broke up, and she was wretched. I heard about it from a third party. I called her up and we had dinner, maybe went to a movie or something like that. At that time if you went out with somebody for dinner you always had breakfast. It started gradually, and it got so we couldn't stand being apart. The reason we weren't going to get married was that she'd be a widow too long.

CD: You've written about that.

DH: I know. I've said it a million times, and it was true enough. As her poetry got better she became beautiful, so that by the time she was forty years old she was a knockout.

CD: That sounds mythological.

DH: She was sort of deliberately not attractive in her face, when she was twenty-three years old, twenty-two years old. In the Eighties, she grew her hair long, and then had it curled. She had a little helmet of hair, and the amazing thing was when she decided to wear lenses to accentuate her beauty. Her new beauty grew with the excellence of the poetry and the success of the poetry.

CD: Well she must have been picking up a huge amount through osmosis, living with you and being around other poets.

DH: We had to get over being teacher and student, which we did, and we helped each other with our work.

CD: There's so little "irritable reaching," as Keats wrote about successful poetry, in Jane's work.

DH: I know. There's a lot of depression, but the language, in a poem about depression, the language loves the world. That she was getting better and better was also an impetus to me. People assume, because of the difference in age, that I particularly helped her, but in the long run I think she helped me just as much.

A couple of days we each had a letter in the mail from a magazine; once it was *The New Yorker*, and one of us had sold a poem and the other had not. What would happen was that the person who should be happy wouldn't act too happy. (Laughs.) We would avoid competition. One thing amused me a lot. When we were first married a couple of people asked us to read together, people who knew I had married a young poet. They didn't know her work, and after about two or three times, she said, "No more, Perkins, we're not going to read together anymore." For years, people would ask us to read together and we'd say, no, but we'll come and we'll do two separate readings. Finally one day we were at a university and one of us had read, and one of us was reading the next night, and at a meeting of the writing program she had ten times as many questions as I did. She said, "Perkins, I think we can read together now."

CD: Is Perkins just a name she came up with?

DH: It's not very interesting, where it came from. We were driving around, exploring, got into Maine and went to Perkins Cove and Jane saw Perkins Avenue, Perkins Drug Store, Dr. Perkins, and she said, "This Perkins must have been quite a fellow." And then she started calling me Perkins. At the time she was my student, nobody called me Professor Hall or Mr. Hall, it was Don. All students would call me Don—that became a teacher's name. So maybe she needed Perkins. I don't know.

CD: It's wonderful to hear those stories. There was an intellectual intimacy you had even before she became a well-known poet.

DH: We were very close and in many ways we were so different. I was an extensive reader and she was an intensive reader. I would read all of Henry Adams, one book after another, and she would read all the poems of Keats, all the letters of Keats, all the good biographies of Keats. Then she'd go back and read the poems of Keats and the letters of Keats, and so on. Her knowledge of English poetry as a long history was not great. But intense. She studied and studied. I don't know if you could trace any Keats in her except in sound. But she wasn't that into writing iambic.

CD: In her last poems there are a lot of biblical references. She wrote a psalm she wanted to leave out of the book.

DH: I know what you mean. It was a wonderful poem called

"Woman, Where Art Thou," a quotation from the Bible. It's about India. I tried to persuade her to print it. When we did the subsequent book of prose, I wanted to print it, so I asked Joyce and Alice, who were her closest friends. They agreed. Peter Davison printed it in *The Atlantic*. I do love that poem.

CD: You both attended the church here, the Congregational Church, so over the years did you develop a strong religious or devotional commitment together?

DH: In Ann Arbor, she hadn't been to a church service since she was nine years old. We came here and on our first Sunday, when we were alone here, I said I think my cousins will expect us to go to church. My dear cousins.

CD: Did your grandparents go to church here?

DH: Same place. I sat in the same pew as my grandparents. Jane said "okay." We went to church and met a band of cousins, great people, Democrats in New Hampshire. The preacher quoted "the great Austrian poet Rilke" in the middle of his service. Everybody was very welcoming and people called me Donny for the first time since I was twelve years old, which melted me. We went back the next week and Jane started to read scripture and several of the mystics. Julian of Norwich was her favorite and typically I went to Meister Eckart. She became intensely religious, but she retained her bawdy side.

CD: This is before she became sick?

DH: Yes. In fact, when she became sick, she seldom spoke of

religion. When she knew she would die, the only thing she said was "I don't fear punishment." Nothing was said about a meeting in the future. She led me in a religious way, as in many ways. I would read her the four gospels every year at Christmas and again at Easter. I read her *The Ambassadors* twice. I read it to her once, and then a year later she wanted to hear it again. The first time I had read it to her she had never read it. Do you remember in *The Ambassadors* when Chad Newsome appeared with his mistress in the boat? Jane was going O, with her mouth.

CD: So there was more reading than television?

DH: She loved baseball to a degree but she never got past the fifth inning, falling asleep. We watched *Mary Hartmann, Mary Hartman*.

CD: Many of your contemporaries—Galway Kinnell, Ruth Stone, Maxine Kumin, Jack Gilbert—have publicly renounced their belief in God. You're unique among them for expressing any formal religious affiliation or belief in God.

DH: Galway has written out of religion so much without believing. I have no conviction that God exists or that there is an afterlife, yet I still go to this church. I love the community of it and the old people. I was still skeptical with Jane, but I was further toward belief at that time, and was a devoted churchgoer.

CD: Did that ever become an issue between you and her?

DH: No.

CD: There was strong respect?

DH: Absolutely. Every time there'd be communion she'd weep.

CD: Jane developed a courageous faith later in life that became an essential aspect of her poetic sensibility as well. One sees this in such poems as "Mosaic of the Nativity: Serbia, Winter 1993," "Man Eating," "Man Sleeping," and "Dutch Interiors."

DH: She knew nothing at the beginning, and had never read the Bible or any part of it. I think certainly not theologians or mystics. She gradually came to it.

CD: With regard to your work ethic, which is a kind of faith, you write this memorable directive in your poem "Kill the Day": "Work, love, build a house and die."

DH: Yes, I got this from the Swabian motto, "Work, work, build a house, die." It was apparently a mocking song about the stability of Swabians. I took it over and added love and made it my own. You've also read "Kill the House"?

CD: Yes.

DH: It's the fourth section of *The One Day*. I don't print it as such because it obviously comes out of Jane's death.

CD: Right, that's a memorable title. In your poem "Deathwork" you write this in the midst of your bardo state:

Pace and curse.
For solitude's support
Drink Taylor's port.

Smoke cigarette.
Sleep. Sweat.
Nightmare until dog whimpers.

My questions after reading this were, Have you felt like death's slave since Jane died, and what specific effect do you feel your deathwork has had on your poetry?

DH: To write about grief at the beginning kept me alive. I'd write an hour or two in the morning about it, and then I'd wait twenty-two hours in misery until I could get back to it. The only thing I felt was pleasure when I was working on these poems. I was obviously trying to embody grief in a particular and hang it out there. I worried about possible sentimentality, and sent it to ten people. Then I worked on it, after their suggestions, and sent it to ten different people. Then I worked on it again and sent it to ten people from the previous twenty, the ones who had been most helpful. People did little things and big things. In a poem called "Weeds and Peonies," I talked about seeing Jane walking Gus and I added "hisgreat tail wagging." Galway Kinnell crossed out "wagging" and put in "swinging." So much better. Also the first section where it's "he" it was originally "I." It looked like palm trees "I," "I," "I" everywhere. One reader, Caroline Finkelstein, said, "Try 'he'." I tried it. The final group of ten, who had seen it before, never objected to the change. Everybody understood it. I felt more urgent getting help on this book because I didn't want to mess anything up, or be sentimental.

CD: I would never have guessed that; it's so much yours. You seem to transcend ambition in many of your recent poems, while simultaneously maintaining your highly developed sense and praxis of craft.

DH: It's as if I had been practicing to write Without my whole life. You know I was not feeling ambitious when I wrote those poems.

CD: You were just mentioning the poem "Kill the Day," which has so many wonderful stanzas in it. I'd like to read a few to you since this poem does such a nice job of capturing both your feelings and philosophy after Jane died.

Now he woke each morning wretched with morning's
regret that he woke. He woke looking forward
to a nap, to a cigarette, to supper, to port measured,
to sleep blessed sleep on the permanent painted bed
of death. Sleep, rage, kill the day, and die.
When she died, he died also. For the first year
his immediate grief confused him into feeling alive.
He endured the grief of a two-month love affair.
When women angry and free generously visited
the frenzy of his erotic grief, melancholia
became ecstasy, then sank under successful dirt.
Without prospect or purpose, who dares to love meat
that will putrefy? He rejoiced that he was meat.
How many times will he die in his own lifetime?
When TWA 800 blew out of the sky, his heart ascended
and exploded in gratitude, finding itself embodied
and broken as fragments scattering into water.
Then little green testicles dropped from the oaks
on New Canada Road again, another August of death,
and autumn McIntoshes rotted on the dwarf trees
already pecked by the loathsome birds of July.

Your grief has focused you here with a vision that has one eye on this world and the other on the next. Nothing like *The One Day* really. And of course the speaker is "he" rather than "I," which provides helpful distance from this intense, philosophical voice.

DH: The end of *The One Day* has the toad standing still. "Kill the Day" began in a fierce depression, an angry depression, about a year and six months after Jane died. I remember one morning in which I walked around with a yellow pad and I wrote something like twenty pages. After a year it turned out to be "Kill the Day."

CD: You reach an ironic point of heroic release in "Affirmation," your last poem in "Throwing Away" in *White Apples and the Taste of Stone*: "Let us stifle under mud at the pond's edge / and affirm that it is fitting / and delicious to lose everything." Why did you put many of the poems that were originally in your book Without under the title "Throwing Away" in *White Apples and the Taste of Stone*?

DH: None of my old books is printed intact in White Apples and the Taste of Stone. I deleted things. I rearranged things. Using the book Without, I printed the parts about the sickness (the "he" parts) under ALL—which is Acute Lymphoblastic Leukemia. Some parts deleted. Then I wanted to use the grief poems separately, some of them from the book after *Without,* others from *The Painted Bed*. I was looking for the right order, deleting parts of each book as ever. I printed the letters in another section.

CD: Your poem "Mount Kearsarge" contains both ethereal and concrete imagery. This is the mountain you have lived beneath since you and Jane moved to Wilmot in 1977. Can you talk about how this mountain has remained such an ongoing inspiration through your joy and grief here at Eagle Pond? I'm particularly struck by how succinctly you wed music to meaning, especially in the last lines: "I turn my back on you, / Kearsarge. I close / my eyes, and you rise inside me, / blue ghost."

DH: "Mount Kearsarge," as the poem makes clear, was written when I visited my grandmother here, knowing that I would never live here. I was wrong. It's a poem of sound, a poem of ecstasy and despair put together. The pale blue mountain ghost. When I wrote that last line, "blue ghost," I did not realize I was taking the second and fourth words from the first line. I was making sound in the poem, and it sounded good, and then I saw what I had done when somebody asked me to talk about the shape of the poem. I read that poem often, because it's something that everyone can get, hearing it aloud. I like making the sound of it.

GALWAY KINNELL

Photo by Richard W. Brown

I met with Galway Kinnell at his home in Sheffield, Vermont on March 7th, 2009. We sat in his rustic, book-filled study on a cold winter day with the wood stove going. Often, long silences punctuated our conversation, which I sometimes mistakenly interrupted. Every half hour or so Galway got up from his desk chair to put another log in the stove. His desktop was covered with heaps of loose poems and open books. He answered my questions deliberately and incisively, but also with a humility and circumspection that indicated there were no final, clear answers to most big questions about one's life or poetry. As the wind blew across the expansive meadow that is his front "yard" and "fairway of the bears," revealing a spectacular view of the White Mountains to the east and the Green Mountains to the west, I asked Galway why he loved living here, his home since 1960. Without pausing, he replied, "The silence."

CD: In his elegy, "In Memory of W. B. Yeats," W. H. Auden addresses the ghost of Yeats, "Mad Ireland hurt you into poetry." Can you, in thinking back on your career, remember what specifically hurt you into poetry?

GK: I don't know. Perhaps the sense of stagnation I felt growing up in a decayed mill town in the Depression, damaged me into poetry.

CD: You write about Pawtucket in several of your poems. One thing that struck me when you visited my creative writing class at Providence College last year was your comment that you were reluctant to call yourself a poet.

GK: A poet should not call himself a "poet." Being a poet is so marvelous an accomplishment that it would be boasting to say it of one's self. I thought this well before I read that Robert Frost took the same view.

CD: Do you think it's dangerous to think of yourself as a poet?

GK: It's not dangerous. One may hope that one is a poet, or even believe it, but it's better all around if someone else declares it.

CD: When did you move to Sheffield?

GK: I bought this old house in 1960. I've lived in it summers and parts of winters. It wasn't until 1995 that I succeeded in making it my permanent home. I liked living half in New York and half in Vermont. I think I might have felt something essential was missing in me if I had lived all the time only in the city or only in the country.

CD: You were writing about your Vermont house at the beginning of your career, and at the same time you were also writing such urban poems as "The Avenue Bearing the Initial of Christ into the New World" and "The River That Is East."

GK: Yes.

CD: I'm hard pressed to think of another American male poet who has written as affectionately and prolifically about his children as you have. You seem in paradise as a father in such poems as "Under the Maud Moon," "Little Sleep's-Head Sprouting Hair in the Moonlight," "Fergus Falling," "After Making Love We Hear Footsteps," "It All Comes Back" and "Everyone Was In Love" even though some of these poems address dark or frightening subjects—the Vietnam War, Fergus falling out of a tree.

GK: To me, being a parent was entirely a joy. I never became angry with my children – and seldom even irked --except one time, when they were jumping around in the back of the car on one of those ten-hour journeys between Sheffield and New York.

CD: This is clear in your poems about them.

GK: It's not as if I wrote only the good parts and left the bad parts out. For me, it was all the good part. I may not have been a good father, in the sense that I traveled a lot during their childhood and adolescence, because that's how I made my living. It put a strain on my wife, and on my marriage, and it wasn't good, but I had to do it, and also, of course, I wanted to do it. They suffered. Suffered is possibly too strong a word, but they didn't like it. Whenever I was invited to go on a long trip somewhere, I explained to them at once what it would entail and asked if it would be okay with them if I did it and they saw it was important to me and said, "Yes, do it." Of course, I realize that their wish to accommodate me prevented them from telling me how much really it would cost them for me to be away for so long.

CD: In almost every book since *The Book of Nightmares* you have included poems about your children. A recent poem from your last book, "It All Comes Back," is a favorite among my students.

GK: I'm glad to hear that.

CD: They love the way the son is father of the man in this poem.

GK: I wanted life to go on in this way forever. They were wonderful children. They didn't play the piano or sing or do anything elaborate, they just were great children. They seldom quarreled and when they did, it was usually over some small thing and usually they settled it themselves. They had an interest in all sorts of things and liked playing together. And I liked the habit they had, right up to college, of using my knees as their favorite chairs, when company came.

CD: In your poem "The Past" from your 1985 book of the same title, you write, "I wanted to sit at the table/ and look up and see the sea spray/ and beach grass happy together./ I wanted to remember the details:/ the dingy, sprouted potatoes,/ the Portuguese bread, the Bokar's coffee,/ the dyed oranges far from home,/ the water tasting of decayed aluminum,/ the kerosene stench." By recollecting random things from your past, you hold on to the past in the present, living twice as it were. This poem appears to be an important apology for the elegiac side of your view of the world, as you claim in the poem yourself: "For of the four/ possibilities—from me-and-it/still-here to it-and-me-/both-gone—this one, me-here-/it-gone, is second best,/ and will do, for me, for now./" I'm curious why you omitted this poem from your last selected poems, especially since it expresses the actual logic of that elegiac side?

GK: Did I leave it out of my selected poems? Well, a "Selected Poems" does not necessarily consist of only the best poems. It is also a sampling of the range of the work. I trust readers, if they like the selected poems, to get other of my books, and possibly discover in them poems they like as well. But if I had known that you liked "The Past" especially, I would have put it in the *New Selected*. For one thing, it is fully unencumbered by religious thinking.

CD: I hope you do salvage it in your next collection. I noticed also while listening to your CD of *Strong Is Your Hold* that you changed and added lines to poems, and even in some cases stanzas.

GK: Yes.

CD: Do you feel that poetry remains an elusive process?

GK: I know that as time passes, some poems that seemed to me rather perfect cease to, and sometimes, maybe even after twenty years, I see what's wrong. So I mark the corrections in a copy of the book. In my library is a corner where the books are labeled "Marked Copy" in heavy ink on the covers.

CD: In the Whitman anthology you edited titled *The Essential Whitman*, you edited several of Whitman's poems by incorporating his most successful changes in the various editions of *Leaves of*

Grass, thus creating new versions of his poems that consisted of his best revisions. Do you feel there are only a fraction of Whitman's complete poems that are, to use a term from Samuel Johnson, "durable"?

GK: If you gave a book of Whitman's final versions of his poems to someone who knew little about poetry but could recognize it, such a person could read and read and find the book extremely uneven. I came upon Whitman in college, but I soon stopped because, like many poets, he wrote so many awful poems, and published all of them. Also, he revised his poems unwisely and made some of his early poems worse. He seems to have lost the capacity to criticize his own work, and come to feel that whatever effused from his being was glorious. As I wandered through his poetry, I encountered so many of Whitman's rotten poems that I gave up – temporarily. Ten years later, I studied his poetry in preparation for teaching a course on Whitman at the University of Grenoble. Suddenly I fell in love with his poems, and he has been my greatest influence ever since. I realized that if one starts by reading very closely Whitman's first book, the unrevised "Song of Myself," one would be obliged to see his genius at once. As far as *The Essential Whitman*, I tried to collect into that book only his best poems in their best versions.

CD: And was Frost another influence? I love your homage to him, where you start off very humorously about his gift for gab, asking, "Why do you talk so much, Robert Frost?" But I don't get the impression that you've actually been that influenced by Frost, despite living in Frost country.

GK: I've never felt an influence from Frost. And I don't really live in Frost country. His was a world of actual, functioning, often prosperous farms, which are long gone from my part of Vermont. But I love Frost's poems. I admire most his poem "Home Burial." To write it must have taken extraordinary self-knowledge and natural truthfulness, as well as the power to enter into the feelings of another, a power not all poets possess. In this poem, I feel that Frost was determined to write the whole truth, and he did. Convincingly. He never surpassed this poem. It concentrates only on reality, and it is free of banter.

CD: "I'll come after you, I will" is such a brutal last line to that poem spoken by the husband.

GK: Edward Thomas, Frost's English friend and poet who was killed in World War I, objected to the harsh ending, but Frost stuck to his guns.

CD: A consistently raw quality runs throughout your work, resounding with primordial energy. It's almost as if you write with dirt in your mouth, figuratively speaking of course.

GK: That's pretty good.

CD: Does this make sense to you?

GK: I don't know, but I like it.

CD: But there's also an agonistic quality in your work that contains both antinomian and metaphysical elements, a quality that is on the one hand Frost-like in its affirmation of Earth being "the right place for love," this visceral, mortal planet where your hunter in "The Bear" discovers "that sticky infusion, that rank flavor of blood, that poetry" by which he lives, and a metaphysical view on the other, a realm beyond this world as you describe it in "Under the Maud Moon" where there is "a sadness/ stranger than ours, all of it/ flowing from the other world."

GK: I wonder if either can exist without the other.

CD: Strong public speakers appear in much of your poetry, as well, from The Book of Nightmares to your poem about 9/11, "When the Towers Fell." Other poets of your generation, Philip Levine, Adrienne Rich, W.S. Merwin, Maxine Kumin have also alternated back and forth between their public and private muses. With regard to your relatively recent poem, "When the Towers Fell," you have credited Paul Celan's poem, "Death Fugue," as an influence. Was Celan's poem a particularly strong influence behind "When the Tower's Fell"?

GK: Well, he was never an influence, as far as I can see, but "Death Fugue" is a poem I've always very much admired. It is a poem "to live by." I wanted to quote bits of it in my own poem.

CD: It's hugely ambitious, as are many of your other prophetic or public poems are, such as, "The Fundamental Project of Technology," "The Avenue Bearing the Initial of C into the World," "The Dead Shall Be Raised Incorruptible," and "Vapor Trail Reflected in the Frog Pond." We live in a time when very few people seem to be listening to poets, or at least taking them very seriously. Perhaps this has always been the case. Auden said "Poetry makes nothing happen" in his elegy for Yeats. But what has compelled you to write your Amos-like jeremiads and lamentations?

GK: I don't think of my "public" poems as prophetic or exceptionally persuasive. I think of most of them as outcries. The number of people who take poetry seriously probably varies with the number of serious poems there are. A poem often makes something happen, but as the reader may appear on the outside the same after it, you could conclude that nothing has happened. I hope the "nothings" that happened in the Iranian people from reading poetry – they are great poetry lovers – carry them into the streets to attempt their brave and probably brief revolution.

CD: You taught English and American literature in Iran for a year. Was that a fulfilling experience?

GK: Well, yes and no. That was an important period of my life. I spent over a year in Iran in 1959 and 1960. I met a great assortment of people. I became friends with well known poets including Nader Naderpour and Farough Faroughzad. Among my friends from other countries were a Japanese, two Frenchmen, an American who knew Iran well, and a Norwegian who spoke fluent Farsi. It's an amazing country – or at least was. Weekly readings in coffee houses by professional reciters of the great poems of the past; miracle plays, performed secretly out in the countryside, being forbidden by the Shah; elaborate underground streams carrying fresh water through the desert; "strength houses" where ancient martial arts were performed; I could go on. For a long while I thought of writing a book called "The Iran I Loved" and including a lot of my photographs and prose, but it would have taken some doing, especially, corralling and identifying the photographs. I didn't write much poetry while I was there, I don't know all the reasons, but one was that so much of it I didn't understand. I wrote a lot of very long letters about Iran. I was writing weekly articles for the English language edition of an Iranian newspaper, and I was ceaselessly traveling around Iran a lot with my camera. At the same time, I was preparing for and teaching two courses at the University of Tehran.

CD: They published your photographs there?

GK: The newspaper published my photographs and descriptions of some aspect of Iran each week in the centerfold of the Sunday paper. They gave me airline tickets for travel, but I didn't trust the upkeep of the airplanes and so drove everywhere in my little quatre chevaux.. The time flew by. As for poetry, I ended up with a lot of descriptive fragments. Back in the States, I did write a novel set in Iran, called *Black Light*.

CD: Did you find the Persian culture inspiring?

GK: I loved the presence around me of an ancient world. The

Shah was trying to modernize Iran, but luckily everywhere the past showed through.

CD: Did you learn any Farsi?

GK: I learned about 500 words but I couldn't speak or write it. I concluded that for a person like me, with a limited power to learn languages, one can't read Farsi unless one already can speak it. As opposed to Spanish, where the written language tells you exactly how to pronounce every word.

CD: Turning back to your own fascinating language, in your book *What a Kingdom it Was* you use a lot of King James phraseology. I'm thinking of such poems as 'The Avenue Bearing the Initial of Christ into the World," 'The Supper After the Last" and "The Dead Shall Rise Incorruptible." But these poems aren't Christian at all, or even religious. They are in fact rife with natural imagery and atheistic conclusions that echo Wallace Steven's pagan credo at the conclusion of "Sunday Morning." So I'm wondering what your rationale was for incorporating Christian references and conceits into several of your own poems in *What a Kingdom It Was*?

GK: The music of *What a Kingdom It Was* might sound a Christian note but not a Christian belief.

CD: These poems I just mentioned end with mortal and pastoral tropes: 'I breathe the shape of your grave in the dirt," from "The Supper After Last," and these last two lines from "To Christ Our Lord," 'The swan spread her wings, cross of the cold north,/ the pattern and mirror of the acts of earth." So rather than there being any mention of heaven or religion, these poems point earthward in their conclusions, away from religious transcendence.

GK: Little by little I stamped out the Christian applications.

CD: In addition to living in Iran, you also lived in several other countries and states. Did you suffer from wanderlust?

GK: No, I take sustenance from wanderlust. To get me out of my rut, to see all I can of the world. When I was fourteen, I read Richard Halliburton's *The Royal Road to Romance* and Harry Franck's *A Vagabond Journey Around the World.* Basically, perhaps, I just wanted, as an earthling, to know as much as I could of the earth. When I hiked for days and days at a time through some of the great Western forests, I didn't always know where I was exactly. Some people might say I was lost. But I wasn't. I am an earthling. This is my home. I watched the positions of the sun. I read the stars. I studied the terrain. And I had a map and a compass in my pocket.

CD: There's a renegade spirit in your adventures as well as your writing. You inject such intense psychic and emotional energy in your poems. Your language emanates it. Do you find a large difference in the energy you expend in your daily living and your writing? You have maintained amazingly high poetic energy in all your books, upping the ante in both your personal and political subject matter with each new collection.

GK: I don't know if I can up the ante again. My energy comes and goes. Without energy, words are flabby. Energy is their air. It is the kind of energy that allows someone like Stanley Kunitz, putting all his bodily capabilities on hold, using every scrap of energy he saved up, to write – until he was 100.

CD: When did you write "The Quick and the Dead," which is in your most recent book? That poem has remarkable intensity.

GK: *Strong Is Your Hold* came out in 2006. I hope it has that intensity.

CD: In your elegies for your sister and your mother, you use the words "elsewhere" and "someplace else" to describe that realm they have crossed over to. In your poem "Promissory Note," you use the word "oblivion" to describe what follows death. These atheistic references remind me of Whitman's musing on death in "Out of the Cradle Endlessly Rocking," where he also resists using religious language to describe the after non-world.

GK: I must have been 18 or 19 when I realized that much of Christianity is made of wishes. When I graduated from college, my mother asked me if there was a heaven. I thought: Who am I to crush her hopes? I said, "I don't know." "What?" she replied rather indignantly, "You spent four years at Princeton and you didn't even learn if there is a heaven!!" In retrospect, I don't think she was hoping that my answer would strengthen her faith, but simply hoping to find the truth.

CD: You've mentioned you held in some scorn poetry workshops and writing courses when you were at Princeton.

GK: Well, not really. There were only a few workshops, taught by R.P. Blackmur and John Berryman; it would be absurd to be scornful of their courses. The true reason I didn't enroll was that I didn't feel my poetry was developed enough. I didn't want to submit work that I already knew was badly flawed. But one of the professors in the English Department, Charles Bell, saw something in my poems. I liked his poems, too, and we developed a wonderful, lifelong poetry friendship, during which our meetings were sometimes very much like workshops.

CD: I don't know when you wrote "Meditation Among the Tombs.' It was pretty early…

GK: It was early, yes.

CD: A stanza such as this, "But if the darkness finds the graves where we/ Were buried under sillions of our past/ Still pointing gloomy crosses at the east,/ And thinks that we were niggard with our bravery,/ Our ghosts if such we have, can say at least/ We were not misers of our misery," seems pretty good to me.

GK: I guess one could find passages of interesting poetry in some of those early poems, but most were awful all the way through.

CD: Well, you found your own way. You went to Rochester for a year, and then taught for two years at Alfred University, then the University of Chicago. You traveled after that throughout the world. You were active in the anti-war movement; you took part in the Civil Rights activities in the South. You seem to have been percolating the whole time.

GK: Yes, I was, most of the time.

CD: I know you've also been influenced by Emily Dickinson. What do you think about her vacillation between faith and skepticism. One minute, death presages oblivion, as she states in "I Felt a Funeral in My Brain" where she feels "wrecked solitary here," then seemingly faithful the next, as in her poem "Of Course I Prayed" where she carries on an intense one-way conversation with God about his absence. But like you, she often seems far too attached to the things of this world to entertain any real notion of heaven. "It is to difficult a Grace/ to justify the Dream," she writes at the conclusion of 569, "I reckon—when I count at all—".

GK: I don't know that it's her attachment to things of this world so much as it's her clear -sightedness. She seems to have been soaked in Christianity in her youth. In her adulthood I'm sure that her Christian usages were mostly ways of speaking. Her sisters and brothers were Christians, but it seems to me – and many others – that Emily was a staunch skeptic.

CD: You use the most particular, insectivorous language in poems about the agents of death, which are also the agents of life. I'm referring to the flies and maggots in such poems as "The Flies" and "The Quick and the Dead." You seem deeply intrigued by these creatures.

GK: Theirs is an impressive world.

CD: There are these stunning lines about those chthonic agents in "The Quick and the Dead": "I know that if no fellow creatures /can force their way in to do the underdigging/ and jiggling and earthing over and mating/ and egg-laying and birthing forth, then for us/ the most that can come to pass/ will be a centuries-long withering down/ to a gowpen of dead dust, and never/ the crawling of new life out of the old/ which is what we have for eternity on earth."

GK: I wonder if Emily would have appreciated this passage given the earthiness of the language.

CD: I wonder how one could presume speak for Emily, but I would like to answer yes, If she like Higginson's natural descriptions, whish she did, going so far as to memorized them, I certainly think she'd like yours. I'm curious to know where you find words like plouters, pronotum, noggles, sloom, drouking, moils, gowpen and dunch. I can't find them in any dictionary.

GK: They're old words that have stuck to my brain as I read about that nether world, and sometimes peeked into it. They're actual words, except perhaps I made up "dunch." "Moils" and "pronotum" are still words in good standing. Others, unfortunately, have passed out of usage. I hate losing them, so I use them. But I use them only when they pay their way, so to speak, when they seem to express things more accurately or more vividly than our contemporary vocabulary. Do you think that happens?

CD: Oh yes, the word "noggles" describing the way a large beetle moves, I see it. In your poem about the wounded snake, "Burning the Brush Pile," the word "hirpled" describes the hitching motion of a hurt snake perfectly. But I did wonder if these words were neologisms?

GK: They are real words, some still used in certain parts of England.

CD: These are wonderfully descriptive words that you have brought back into the language. Not just one or two, but dozens.

GK: Well, I wish I had in fact brought some of them back. I see no sign of it.

CD: They must have been used by somebody.

GK: There is a *Webster's* dictionary that includes a huge number of the words that have fallen off the back end of the language. Being old, it does not of course include many of the new words. The OED is quite good when it comes to old words. But this Webster's I just mentioned, *The Webster's International*, 1925 edition, may be even better.

CD: I have to say it looks fantastic.

GK: It looks like an ordinary old Webster's but it's considerably fatter.

CD: Looks like a sacred book.

GK: Yes, it is a sacred book. And when you open it, you find lovely pictures and illustrations. It has a weakness for snakes and skulls.

CD: Here's the word "cere" you use in your poem "Ode and Elegy" about the hawk. "The cere above the hawk's beak/ flushes hard yellow from exertion." But this word may still be used to describe, as it says here on my Web dictionary, "the fleshy, membranous covering of the base of the upper mandible of a bird, esp. a bird of prey or a parrot, through which the nostrils open."

GK: It is still used by birders. What I wanted to point out especially about the dictionary is that each page is divided horizontally, into two, a top section for words in use, a bottom section, in smaller print, for words that are out of use.

CD: This is amazing, so much more satisfying than looking up words on Dictionary.com.

GK: I would be surprised if the computer, with its attention focused on the front end of the language, would reach for many of these disappearing words. Now, see, hirples: "to walk with a cramp."

CD: I'm not sure how you first found this word, even in this dictionary.

GK: I must have stumbled across it somewhere.

CD: Where did you get this dictionary?

GK: In a bookstore. One that specialized in used dictionaries and encyclopedias. That kind of bookstore doesn't exist anymore.

CD: I'm going to get one. I could use one. We didn't talk about your translations.

GK: Well, you know we could sit here for the rest of our lives…

CD: But who would feed the chickens?

GK: And we would suddenly wake up twenty years from now and wonder…

CD: Which reminds me of these lines of yours: “Then I will go back/ to that silent evening, where the past just managed/ to overlap the future, if only by a trace,/ and the light doubles and casts/ through the dark a sparkling that heavens the earth.”

One last question. In the last poem of *Strong Is Your Hold,* a poem titled “Why Regret,” you write, “Doesn’t it outdo the pleasures of the brilliant concert/ to wake in the night and find ourselves holding hands in our sleep.” These are actually the last two lines of the poem. They make the valiant claim about what means most to you, not the brilliant concert, or perhaps poem also by implication, but waking in the middle of the night to find yourself holding hands with your beloved.

GK: Is it a valiant claim, or is it a wonderful, surprising realization? Isn’t to find in a moment that we, who chose years ago to live as a couple, are still thrilled to be with each other, isn’t that about the most blessed thing of all?

CD: Yes, and especially heartening to hear from someone who has achieved as much as you as a poet.

GK: Art is wonderful, but the moment love is smashed, darkness falls, deafness falls, nothing survives as it was.

ROBERT AND RUTH BLY

The morning I arrived at Robert Bly's house in Minneapolis on April 21st, 2010, I had just visited my dying father for a week in Detroit Lakes, Minnesota. When I told Robert this he took an immediate, compassionate interest in my father, who was close to his age. I told him a little about his life as a surgeon in Lynchburg, Virginia, Crookston, Minnesota, and Riyadh, Saudi Arabia. Although he and my father had pursued different careers and had few similar interests, Robert felt an immediate camaraderie with him by virtue of their mutual experience as children of the depression. He wanted to know what branch of the military my father had served in and where he had gone to college and who my mother was and whether my father was still married to her. All questions I was happy to answer. In fact, I enjoyed this role reversal, needing to tell someone the salient details of my father's life after just seeing him so near death. Robert must have sensed this and obliged me, while also satisfying his curiosity about a fellow member of his generation, as if he were a long lost brother. Robert and his wife Ruth invited me into their stately, Victorian home on Gerard St., showed me to their living room and fixed me a cup of a tea. Robert had spent the previous day and evening with his children and grandchildren, so he was more tired than he expected he would be. I began asking him several general questions about his multifaceted career, but soon realized that he seemed both distracted and restless. After about half an hour of rambling from one topic to another, Robert confessed that he wasn't feeling "very sharp" this morning and needed a nap. "Could you come back tomorrow?" he asked. I told him I was flying back to

Vermont the following day at 6 in the morning. “Well then, do you mind coming back this afternoon some time?” he suggested. “Not at all.” I replied. Ruth then invited me to make myself at home in the living room until Robert awoke from his nap. I assured her I had enough school work to keep me busy. For the next four hours I read back over many of Robert’s poems and graded papers while Robert slept upstairs and Ruth worked around the house. Suddenly around eleven o’clock I heard loud moose-like bellows emanating from upstairs. Ruth appeared in the living room and said, “Robert’s awake. He should be down shortly. He always makes those noises when he’s waking up.” Within the next few minutes Robert descended the stairway leading to the foyer beside the living room. “Now where were we?” he asked, appearing much sharper. He then asked Ruth to join us. In the time I had been waiting for Robert to return, I decided that the best place to restart the interview would be with his recent poems. So that’s where we began anew, proceeding from there to topics that arose naturally from his poems and led to conversation that didn’t seem possible when we had first sat down four hours earlier.

CD: Good morning, Robert. Would you mind starting this interview with a recent poem?

RB:

You and I have spent so many hours working.
We have paid dearly for the life we have.
It’s all right if we do nothing tonight.

We’ve heard the fiddlers tuning their old fiddles,
And the singer urging the low notes to come.

We've heard her trying to keep the dawn from breaking.

There's some slowness in life that is right for us,
But we love to remember the way the soul leaps
Over and over into the lonely heavens.

CD: Wonderful.

RB: There are good o's in there. "But we love to remember the way the soul leaps over and over into the lonely heavens."

CD: Yes.

RB: What do you think? I love it.

CD: Me too. In 1963 you argued against the "old position," as you called it, of academic poetry, championing instead European and South American poets, poets such as Neruda, Trakl, Vallejo, Machado, Ponge, Ekelof, Jimenez and Rilke. Do you think the influence of these poets, many of whom you translated in your magazine *The Fifties and The Sixties*, have ended up transforming contemporary American poetry in a lasting way, beyond, say, the influence this poetry had on you and James Wright specifically?

RB: (to Ruth Bly) What do you think?

Ruth Bly: Well, I think you could say that among the small faction of people who care about poetry, there has been a change. There are a great many more poets now, but most of them have no idea of the poets you named. They could learn. Is that right?

RB: That's right, but I do think that the attention to European poetry has changed American poetry and made it less rigid and more playful. So I don't feel bad about that. I feel good about that.

CD: James Wright quoted your phrase "new imagination" in a 1958 letter to you, referring to the new free verse poetry he was about to embark on, but he hadn't yet given himself full license, as you already had, to write evocative, often surreal free verse.

RB: I suppose that's right.

CD: He wrote to you, "I mentioned having written a farewell to poetry even before I saw *The Fifties*. Now it may turn out that I do indeed have nothing in the way of vision and imagination but I am stuck now, if I have nothing I'm convinced that I can face the fact without bitterness. The new imagination is so important to all living human beings and not just the literati, that I am going to continue to search for it and if I cannot find it myself then I will identify and fight for it in others. And this is not mock humility: I see blood in this matter, too." This is from one of James Wright's letters that his widow Annie Wright published in her 2005 collection of Wright's letters titled *A Wild Perfection, the Selected Letters of James Wright*.

RB: Wonderful. Wonderful.

CD: Does that bring back a clear sense of what you were both up to at the time, I mean your attempt to rejuvenate American poetry through translating many unknown European poets into English, and then emulating their surrealistic styles?

RB: Yes, it does. And it's wonderful, his passion here, and his willingness to offer himself. Beautiful.

CD: Yes. Could you define now what you meant exactly by the "new imagination"?

RB: Well, I think, you know, clumsily, it's described as an imagination which allows the unconscious to come in with its various ignorances and brilliances. And when Jim and I grew up, the poems, as in the *Kenyon Review*, were well controlled by the rational part of the mind which had only a little bit of playfulness. But that's a little different than letting the wolf in the house.

CD: Yes.

RB: And I think that was Jim's longing, and my longing as well, to let the dogs in the house and let the wolves in the house as long as they don't ruin it, and get a little bit of life going.

CD: And you felt that the new critics had kept the wolves out.

RB: Yes. Neruda let the wolves in, fed them from his own plate.

CD: So did you. But would you call Wright's poetry playful?

RB: Yes, I think I would. His poem "Lying in the Hammock on William Duffy's Farm in Pine Island, Minnesota" is really playful.

CD: And risky too. I love what Ed Ochester says about the penultimate line of that poem where he refers to the hawk "looking for home." He made the following observation to me recently in an email: "My point about that poem's last lines is that the speaker's assertion about the hawk 'looking for home' is so wrong/sentimental (the hawk is looking for something to kill & eat) that it suggests the speaker's obsession. . . .I wonder sometimes if Wright's longing for home didn't include some sense of betrayal caused by his success. I live in Appalachia and I see all the time how those left behind here have mixed feelings about those who've left--it's not just jealousy, but a sense that some bond or fraternity has been betrayed; see how the speaker, Wright, talks in two voices (the learned poet and the down home boy) to that good man the scoutmaster Ralph Neal in 'The Flying Eagles' prose poem."

RB: Yeah, there are a lot of people who have written about that line, "I have wasted my life," but they say that if he's written a poem like that, how could he have wasted his life? That misses the point.

CD: You have made the following observation about Wright in an essay you wrote about him: "The question the poem never asks directly is this: how is it possible for there to be so many spiritual emblems, signs, reminders of the path everywhere, and yet for the man who sees them to have gotten nowhere, to have achieved none of the spiritual tasks that those emblems suggest?" Do you feel as you write later in this same essay that "there is a sense of a vague and shifting ego underneath."

RB: Surely that is true of all of us.

CD: With regard to your own poems, there is confident playfulness that often pervades your own writing about the self and ego, as in these lines from your recent poem that appeared in the January/ February issue of *The American Poetry Review*. "Let's just agree we're on our own now,/ And that we have to wash our own pajamas./

And figure out some way to get to Greece."

RB: Well, maybe we have to go back a hundred years and recite some of Wordsworth's sonnets back to him.

CD: (laughing) What did you mean by that, that it might be important for him to hear his own poems?

RB: I guess it would interrupt his walking if we were to recite some of his sonnets back to him. He probably preferred walking.

CD: And your other poem from this same issue of APR, "Nirmala's Music" is also playful.

RB: (Reading "Nirmala's Music")

"And women suffer the most. Between every child born,
So many rugs are woven and taken apart. The water
Of a hundred bowls is poured on the ground.

The hungry tigers follow the disappearing dogs
Into the woods of life. Women understand this,
For this is a world in which everything is lost."

CD: What do we have to do to come to the same understanding?

RB: Well, you know, we have to stop denying that the dogs are disappearing.

CD: I see.

RB: Didn't we used to have more dogs around here? Images are so fantastic, aren't they? You just put them down and they run off on their own somewhere.

CD: Do you write your dreams down?

RB: I do, sometimes.

CD: Do you ever write from those?

RB: Not much, but I do believe the dreamer is more intelligent than we are. Bold, I should say. Bold, bold. The dreamer is very bold.

CD: Even in his unconscious state?

RB: Yes. The dreamer says, "I'll show you something that will curl your hair."

CD: This reminds me of a remark you made about Tomas Transtromer, that he's unbelievably fast, "like some runner… who enters the forest and suddenly, he's gone. He's ahead of you. I don't know where he is. Forest flower, flowers from a silent search party after something that has disappeared in the dark. It's not a teasing thing exactly, but there's a feeling that Transtromer's closer to some silent energy in the middle of the universe than the rest of us are."

RB: Good.

CD: You go on.

"Things not yet happened are already here.

I feel that they're just out there, the murmuring mass outside the
barrier.
They can only slip in one by one. They want to slip in.
Why? They do, one by one.
I am the turnstile."

RB: I remember that. But what does it mean?

CD: It's very similar to what you were saying about the dreamer. People think of you as having many careers: poet, leader of the men's movement, gadfly and critic of the government, especially during the Vietnam and Iraqi wars, author of such nationally resonant socio/psychological books as *Iron John, The Maiden King* and *The Sibling Society*, founder of the Great Mother Conference, translator extraordinaire. I'm wondering in looking back on your multifaceted career if you see how all these disciplines and works as part of the same enterprise or as separate projects?

RB: They're all separate for me, but each is a form of troublemaking.

CD: You're a troublemaker.

RB: Yeah. Troublemaker in the inward world, I suppose.

CD: You've always been this way.

RB: Probably that's right.

CD: Your response to Archibald McLeash when you were at Harvard is a good example of your trouble-making. He said to you one day after calling you into his office, “Robert, either you’re going to have to start behaving in class or I’m going to jump out the window.”

RB: (Laughing) I said, “Okay, jump.”

CD: I heard you once placed T.S. Eliot’s hat on his head at a party rather than merely handing it to him.

RB: Yes.

CD: Did you have that attitude because you had just come back from the war and were feeling invincible and rebellious, or was it in you all along?

RB: What sort of attitude?

CD: Well, that mischief-making attitude that compelled you to mistrust the establishment and fight it, just as you later rebelled against rationalistic, conscious thinking in much of the formal, academic poetry of the fifties.

RB: Yeah, irreverent in a way. But irreverent as if, among friends. Yes, I remember putting the hat on Eliot’s head and pulling it down. We were just leaving the party, and he was very proper, and he said, mildly, “Well, you know every man likes to put on his own hat.”

CD: How did you feel about Eliot at that point? That was, what the early ‘60s?

RB: Oh, he was so enormous and so fantastic.

CD: Yes. Turning to a title that reminds me of one of Eliot's flood subjects, especially in *Four Quartets,* I'm curious about where you got the title for your book, *What Have I Ever Lost by Dying*.

RB: It comes from the end of one of Rumi's poems.

"I lived for thousands and thousands of years as a mineral,
   and then I died and became a plant.
And I lived for thousands and thousands of years as a plant
   and then I died and became an animal.
And I lived for thousands and thousands of years as an animal
   and then I died and became a human being.
Tell me, what have I ever lost by dying?"

CD: Do you remember how you came to that?

RB: Well, dying is something we are doing all our life.

CD: You then talk about loss of the ego. And yet you have such a strong identity as a person.

RB: You have to be a good captain if you're going to get your boat through the rapids.

Ruth Bly: Well, how did you protect your time for writing poetry? How did you do that?

CD: That's a good question.

RB: Well, by not teaching in the first years of thinking for myself.

Ruth Bly: What else?

RB: What do you think? How did I protect my time?

Ruth Bly: You had a fantastic ability to do that.

RB: Well, it happened that I enjoyed reading poetry aloud and learned to let my poetry penetrate the audience. I was able to make a living without teaching all day. I'd teach once a week or something like that. It was just a gift from God, that's all.

CD: So solitude has obviously been essential for you.

RB: Yes. I suddenly thought of that little poem, driving home from Ortonville…

CD: Do you have it?

RB: So, one thing that I did is, you know, I wasn't content with just living, I wanted to mess up the literary world.

CD: You did a good job!

RB: And so, lots of letters and stuff would come in, and it began to disturb me. I had a little shack by the lake, about 30 miles from home, and I would drive there, and there was nothing there, really. Nothing there but the lake and a few poems and I'd spend all day there, and so, you know, there's a blessing in immersing yourself in the life of the culture or something like that. There's a blessing in giving poetry meaning and seeing how your poems actually hear… sound when you say them out loud. So I had an ability to speak things aloud. I don't know how I received that, since my father was such an introvert. I think it's just the love of poetry that made me want to hear it spoken and see it in people's faces. That love was a gift, but somehow one needs cunning as well because the world is very hypnotic and greedy. I asked the world to invade my house and it did. And then, what do I do about that? If you have children, even more noise. So I got this tiny cabin, and I'd go there by myself and have a little place where no one knew where I was, and I could be sort of destitute again, alone. So, that solitude was a blessing and it's something that the people who teach in universities often don't get. I've always wanted to teach in a university, because I love teaching. But on the other hand, then my world would be a social world, but if you have a solitary cabin, then it's a nature world.

CD: There really have been these two extremes in your life, of being so amazingly social in your work with men's groups, your poetry readings, and your protests during the Vietnam and Iraqi wars, and then there are these times as well of great seclusion and isolation throughout your life from which your poetry seems to emerge.

RB: But again, you see that that's one benefit of not teaching at a university, where you're sort of pushed into a social life every day. It worries me that so many poets teach in a university.

CD: Yes. I'm one of them.

RB: My father was smart enough to buy two farms besides his own, one of which he gave to my brother who wanted to be a farmer, and the other to me, who didn't want to be a farmer. So somehow there were both impulses in him. He didn't judge me for not wanting to be a farmer.

CD: I see.

RB: And I suppose he would have loved it if his father had been able to do something like that for him. So I think that in some way, his straightforward, heavily guarded, masculine concentration was good for me in the end, and showed that even the hard-working masculine stuff can have a blessing for the introverted son.

CD: Even though you were not always introverted.

RB: That's right.

CD: How was your father affected by your work, your decision to become a poet?

RB: Well, he certainly never opposed my being a writer. He himself was in school in Minnesota when his own father died. He had to come home and take over the farm, so he had soft place in his heart for a son who could do what he wanted to do. He was a wonderful father in that respect.

CD: He was always supportive of you as a writer?

RB: He did say once, very mildly, because I didn't have any money and I wasn't eating very much, "Maybe if you ate regularly you'd be able to work a little more."

CD: Is that when you were hunting partridge for food?

RB: Yes, that's right. And I said, "No, I don't think so," and he gave in right away.

CD: After graduating from Harvard you lived off your wits in New York City, painting part time, then moving back to Minnesota and living on your farm, but not farming.

RB: Yes, in New York I earned some money painting. The man in the agency who arranged painting jobs took a liking to me for some reason. He knew I was trying to be a writer. So he said, "There's a place out in Brooklyn, a huge building the owner wants painted inside. You go out there and do as much as you want every day, and if you want to quit and do your writing, that's all right, and I'll just tell the owner something else happened and they should have patience." Wonderful…I mean you meet people like that who need steady work, but are perfectly happy to help some lonely writer. I'm amazed by that. No jealousy.

CD: Yes indeed. That was a significant amount of time of living on your own, in a very solitary way, after college. Was that period as much of a preparation for you, in an ironic sense, for starting your writing career as going to the Iowa Writers Workshop and studying creative writing in a formal way?

RB: Well, I didn't have much faith in the writing programs, so I probably did better alone, trudging along. I never felt bitter or abandoned. I need a lot of time to brood on things and write bad poems and throw them away.

CD: After establishing yourself as a poet, critic and translator, you turned in the early eighties to facilitating men's groups and writing such books as *Iron John* and *The Sibling Society* that address in prose the dearth of emotional and mythological vocabulary among men in America. There's a men's group you inspired in Providence where I teach that has met on a monthly basis for over 25 years. One of it's members, a friend of mine who works in the Providence College library, asked me to ask you what you think the best way is for men to express their anger today. This is a recurring theme in their group, which was inspired by your ideas at the start of the "expressive men's movement" that you founded in the mid eighties.

RB: What's their problem? Why don't they express it to each other or the person with whom they're angry?

CD: They simply seem at a loss for how to express their anger in a constructive way.

RB: Of course that means they can't express their anger at home. That's one reason for having men's groups. Many times their anger is too powerful for their wives or children, and men can absorb a lot of anger from each other if it's done in a playful way, which it often is. So that's one of the main functions of men's groups, to keep their wives and children safe, and help them get all the stuff out that they've never been able to say to their fathers.

CD: You've talked a lot about shame as one of the main causes for men's anger, and you've written about this too in both Iron John and your poems, especially those about your own father.

RB: Well, why are men ashamed of being ashamed?

CD: That's a good question, but I think it is a problem. If a wife or girl friend says something to her husband or boyfriend about a flaw or an error, even in a jocular way, they often feel profoundly ashamed.

RB: Well, women, you know, frequently confess all sorts of things to each other, and manage to keep self-respect, while the men tend to hold it in.

CD: Why do you think men lack the emotional vocabulary of women?

RB: I think their brains are different for one thing. Women receive permission to be with each other and fight through things and so on, while men feel they have to conquer the world.

CD: And not talk about it?

RB: Right. It's a terrible burden. I've noticed to my terrific surprise when men in a men's group—whether it's a hundred men or ten men—give each other permission, which they intuit, to express their anger, they are so amazed at how easy it is to do, and how the other men are not going to fall over and die, but simply say, "Yes, you did that pretty well. Some good metaphors there."

CD: Do you think the drumming you provide at these settings, particularly the Great Mother Conference you direct each year in Maine, is helpful in creating the right atmosphere for men to express their anger?

RB: Yeah, probably. And of course men have an old link to drumming. You just start them on it and suddenly they go back five hundred years and do some really beautiful rhythms.

CD: And that often acts as a catalyst for singing or talking in some way they might otherwise not do?

RB: Yeah.

CD: If you go back to some of the most ancient texts, such as *Gilgamesh*, Catullus's elegy for his brother and the keening at the conclusion of *Beowulf*, there are such moving passages on grief especially. I especially love Herbert Mason's translation of the chorus's excursus of grief in *Gilgamesh*. After Enkidu dies, the chorus chants, "All that is left to one who grieves/ Is convalescence. No change of heart or spiritual/ Conversion, for the heart has changed/ And the spirit has converted/ To a thing that sees/ How much it costs to lose a friend it loved." So there's this memorable intimacy among men in so many classical texts. When do you think men stopped writing such moving language about their losses?

RB: Well, I think that when the country widens and becomes a larger community, men tend to feel ashamed to be a part of that larger community and think they are unable to express a lot of their grief. I think it's still true that when men get together and give each other permission, material comes out that never would come out in any other way, and a lot of anger is really a lot of bottled up grief that they haven't been able to express. Many women don't know how to influence the flow of that.

CD: Turning back to your career for a moment, which has really been a fulfillment of what Robert Frost envisioned at the conclusion of his poem "Two Tramps in Mud Time" as the ideal life in which one unites his avocation with his vocation as "two eyes make one in sight." How did you, if you don't mind me asking, manage to make a living as a poet while not teaching or working at something else?

Ruth Bly: He went out months at a time.

RB: Yeah.

Ruth Bly: I mean, you'd be gone a month and come home, go to bed sick, and get up, and go out for a month and go back to bed sick, and over and over and over again.

CD: What kind of sickness?

Ruth Bly: He would just be exhausted. He would stay in bed for a while and then get up and go again. Nobody I had ever met had energy like that.

CD: But it would exhaust him.

Ruth Bly: But he wasn't exhausted while he was working. That takes a kind of courage. He worked harder than anybody I've ever met.

RB: Really?

Ruth Bly: Just last year or so, you have taken to sitting, looking out the window, which I think is quite a nice change for you.

CD: Well, it's showing up in your poems in a good way also.

Ruth Bly: Yes.

CD: There's a calmness in your new poems, a new level of wisdom and…

Ruth Bly: An acceptance.

CD: That tone of acceptance emanates from those two poems, “The Threshers” and “Nirmala’s Music” we read earlier on the back of the 2010 March/April issue of APR, as well as from your poem “I Have Daughters and I Have Sons” which appeared in last week’s New Yorker. You appear freed up in a new way in these poems to ask yourself such bold, reflective questions. “Do I ever write to my own poems? Do I ever joke? Do I ever write to my own desires?”

RB: Is that in that poem?

CD: It’s right here.

RB: “At this age, I especially love dawn/ On the sea, stars above the trees,/ Pages in ‘The Threefold Life,’/ And the pale faces of baby mice.”

CD: You’ve always talked about holding creatures to your cheek.

RB: Yes. (Continuing to read from “I Have Daughters and I Have Sons”) “I’ve always loved Yeats’ fierceness/ As he jumped into a poem,/ And that lovely calm in my father’s/ Hands as he buttoned his coat.” Oh goody, goody, goody. That’s pretty good!

CD: I see you’re looking back on this with some joy.

RB: Yeah.

CD: Why?

RB: It took me a long time to write that damn poem.

CD: Do you remember what you were thinking, or what your strategy was when you were writing it.

RB: No. But I made a decision to write it in four stanzas, and you have to keep changing the subject matter if you're going to keep the poem alive.

CD: A little bit ghazal-like, isn't it?

RB: Yes. That's right.

CD: The ghazal has been so important to you for this reason, for being able to change so many horses midstream and still make it across.

RB: Yes. Well, you know the ghazal is made up of several thoughts, and so one gets used to handling it. The sonnet has a nice shape and comes together at the end, but in a ghazal you keep on adding more material.

CD: In talking about the ghazal you remarked in a recent interview that "it often makes a leap to a new subject matter with each new stanza that is, itself, a form of wildness. " But then you go on to say that "the ghazal must have massive forms of discipline to balance that wildness."

RB: Yes.

CD: And you practice that discipline. You have always talked about the domestic and the wild. There's so much poetry being written today that has a kind of wildness to it, or innovation. I was wondering what you think of the lack of what you call discipline in a lot of recent experimental poetry, such new modes as L-A-N-G-U-A-G-E and post avant poetry.

RB: It's pitiful.

CD: Pitiful?

RB: Pitiful.

CD: That's what I thought you'd say.

RB: Yes. There's nothing evil about discipline, as long as you can keep the wildness going. You know, some people are wild with nothing to be wild about.

CD: Right.

RB: And so, that's one reason for saying that someone writing poetry needs to do a lot of reading, so you have something to be wild about.

CD: A lot of your wildness seems to emanate from what Wright said about "the new imagination," a term you coined in one of your first issues of "The Fifties." About ten years after you returned from WW II, you discovered the poetry of several major European Modernists. You were angry and excited at the same time, which seems to have unleashed a wildness in you that hasn't ended to this day.

RB: (Laughing) That's good.

CD: You were going to read that poem about driving back from Ortonville.

RB: Was I? Which one? What are we looking for?

Ruth Bly: I don't know…

CD: The one about driving back from Ortonville.

RB: What else do you remember about it?

Ruth Bly: You have quite a few poems about driving here and there, so I'm not sure.

CD: How about reading any poem you think pertains to what we were just talking about?

RB: Here's one.

Ocean light as we wake reminds us how dark
Our old house is. That's home. Like Hamlet,
One visit to Wittenberg is enough, and we'll soon be
Back in crazy Denmark. I dreamt I stood

In a machine shop; my dead father stands beside me.
We talk, but his eyes remain on my chest.
I say to him for the first time: "Oh look at me
When we talk." I could see cubbyholes

With dark tools, and a rough floor stained with oil.
Clotted windows, cobwebs, a black vise.

But sunlight outside our window speaks of ocean
Light, bone light, Labrador light, prairie light.

It's the same light that glints off swords, and shines
From Idaho river some days, and from the thin
Face just before death. I say to my father,
"We could be there if we could lift our eyes."

CD: What's that one called?

RB: "Words A Dreamer Spoke to my Father in Maine." The dreamer said to my father, "We could be there if we could lift our eyes." "My dead father stood beside me,/ But his eyes remained on my chest.// I say to him for the first time, "Oh look at me when we talk."

CD: I just returned from seeing my father in a state where he couldn't respond to me for the first time.

RB: He couldn't respond to you?

CD: Because of his recent strokes. He doesn't have long to live and is now in a nursing home in Detroit Lakes, Minnesota. But he could lift his eyes to look at me thank goodness. What were you thinking here?

RB: Um…

CD: It's a courageous poem.

RB: Yeah. I say to my father, "We could be there if we could lift our eyes." So the good part is when I say, "We could be there if you'd just lift your eyes." But they both do the same thing I guess.

CD: Do you know why?

RB: (pauses) Mmm…

CD: Why is it so hard for fathers and sons to look each other in the eye?

RB: (pauses) I guess it's something masculine here about eyes meeting and that could be challenging.

CD: But wanting that more than anything.

RB: Boy, some of these are good; they're good in the sense they touch old griefs.… Here's another, "When My Dead Father Called."

Last night I dreamt my father called to us.
He was stuck somewhere. It took us
A long time to dress, I don't know why.
The night was snowy; there were long, black roads.

Finally, we reached the little town, Bellingham.
There he stood, by a streetlamp in cold wind,
Snow blowing along the sidewalk. I noticed
The uneven sort of shoes that the men wore

In the early Forties…

Isn't that amazing how the dreamer would get details like that?

CD: It is.

RB: (Continuing to read)

I noticed
The uneven sort of shoes that the men wore

In the early Forties. And overalls. He was smoking.
Why did it take us so long to get going? Perhaps
He left us somewhere once, or did I simply
Forget he was alone in winter in some town?

Well, I'm glad I did those poems.

CD: Me too.

RB: Alright, well why don't you ask me something else and I'll try to give you an answer.

CD: Let's see, here's a question from the father of one of my students who heard I was going to meet with you and has been meeting in a men's group you inspired in Rhode Island. He wants to know how important you think it is for a man to believe in God for the purpose of successfully completing the masculine journey?

RB: (to Ruth Bly) What do you say?

Ruth Bly: (Laughing) I think you should answer this one.

RB: Well, I don't think anyone can complete the ultimate, masculine journey anyway. But, you know, "believing in God," I don't know exactly what that means. But believing in God certainly means believing that the divine has a role in the world.

CD: I remember Bill Moyers asking Joseph Campbell this question, and Joseph Campbell responding, “I don’t pose the question that way. I believe in the experience of being alive.”

Ruth Bly: (to RB) Well, I think that your answer was more true to what you actually do believe.

RB: What’s my answer?

Ruth Bly: What you just said.

RB: What was it?

CD: About the divine?

Ruth Bly: Yes, the divine definitely has been deep in your work, especially in the last twenty years.

CD: What, the presence of the divine in the world?

Ruth Bly: The presence of the divine everywhere.

CD: Everywhere?

Ruth Bly: One’s ability to understand love.

RB: That’s why Rilke is such a great poet.

CD: Well there’s that Sufi saying, "Everywhere you look, there is the face of God.”

RB : Wherever you look, there's the face of God? Well, I don't know what to say because I think that everyone when they're young recognizes God in the world; it's as natural as the sunlight on trees or something like that. And so you have to go through a lot of labor to get rid of that, and I suppose going to school helps, but for someone like me, it's very stubborn to want to hold onto that.

CD: Why?

RB: Well, it's like believing in your own toes. I mean…(to Ruth) What do you say?

Ruth Bly: Well, all the work that you have done outside of poetry has been to understand the relationship with the divine. I mean that's where you spend most of your thought.

RB: Really?

Ruth Bly: In what's left over from your poetry.

RB: Yeah, so…if poetry doesn't have something to do with the divine, it's not moving.

Ruth Bly: And your ghazals were inspired by reading Gomshei.

RB: That's interesting…that the ghazals, I think, ask for some nod to God in the very last stanza, don't they?

Ruth Bly: Well, some do.

RB: Some do? See our old teacher up there, Dr. Nurbahksh (pointing to a picture on the mantle above the fire place).

CD: Yes. Intense eyes.

RB: Yeah. He had a place in England.

CD: What did he teach?

RB: He was a Sufi. A classic Sufi. He left Iran for political reasons and went to England. A wonderful, wonderful teacher, very mischievous. Never gave you a straight answer to anything. You know the concept of the word nafs?

CD: No.

RB: It refers roughly to the ego and the desirous soul. I said to him one day, “I think my nafs is large, like a truck.” And he said, “No, no, your nafs is a 12 wheeler.” He represented the best of the culture of Iran. I just thought he was marvelous.

CD: Very intense eyes. Well, as far as your own religious background is concerned, you must have grown up Lutheran.

RB: Yes.

CD: Going to Sunday school and all that. And then you branched out, so enormously throughout your life, studying Sufism, Jung; the divine has been in your poetry as a subject, passion and energy that nonetheless has always had an unsayable quiet behind it.

RB: Yes.

CD: Do you still go to church?

RB: Sure. Occasionally I do.

CD: So your specific tradition of Lutheranism has been broad enough for you to branch out, without feeling…

RB: (to Ruth) Why are you shaking your head?

Ruth Bly: It's not so. It's not broad at all. He just broke out of it and added in the Greek gods, and the Indian gods and…

CD: Buddha?

Ruth Bly: Well, not so much Buddha, but certainly the Indians for many years.

RB: Yes. Well, in translating Indian poetry, you just can't escape from the reality that all these poets believe in God, you know, you just can't. It's impossible.

Ruth Bly: And the Mother Conference, which has been going on for 35 years, began with investigations of the goddesses.

RB: The Great Mother, yes.

Ruth Bly: That was not an intellectual investigation.

RB: Yes, I guess so.

Ruth Bly: It couldn't be contained.

RB: What?

Ruth Bly: It couldn't be contained in the forms that we already knew.

CD: And yet, you still find something meaningful about the Lutheran tradition?

RB: Well, certainly. It's better than a poke in the eye with a sharp stick. What else would you like to ask before we go to lunch?

CD: You've said a lot.

RB: If only it were true, you know.

CD: If only it were true?

RB: If only what I said were true.

CD: You know what I'd love for you to do in closing, if you don't mind, is read a few poems that you've written recently.

Ruth Bly: Let's find the newest manuscript, because they're so wonderful, and you could read a couple that are finished.

RB: Alright. Good.

RB: Here's one called "The Roof Nail", four lines. It begins, "A hundred boats are still looking for shore." Is that true?

CD: A hundred boats are still looking for shore?

RB:
A hundred boats are still looking for shore.
There is more in my hopes than I'd imagined.
The tiny roof nail lies in the ground, aching for the roof.
Some little bone in our foot is longing for heaven.

CD: You continue to make wonderful leaps.

RB: Is that true?

CD: Yes.

RB: "Some little bone in our foot is longing for heaven."

CD: Yes, that connection between the nail and the little bone works nicely.

RB: Yes. Good, good, good.

CD: Yes.

RB: Here's another one.

You're alone. Then there's a knock
On the door. It's a word. You
Bring it in. Things go
OK for a while. But this word

Has relatives. Soon
They turn up. None of them work.
They sleep on the floor, and they steal
Your tennis shoes.

You started it; you weren't
Content to leave things alone.
Now the den is a mess, and the
Remote is gone.

That's what being married
Is like! You never receive your
Wife only, but the
Madness of her family.

Now see what's happened?
Where is your car? You won't
Be able to find
The keys for a week.

CD: Wonderful.

RB: (Laughing) Here's another.

Some days we are passive, listening to the incoming waves.
On other days, we are like a light that sweeps
Out over the husky soybean fields all night.

What did we see today? Horses at the end
Of their tethering ropes, the wing of affection going over,
Flying bulls glimpsed passing the moon disc.

Rather than arguing about whether Giordano Bruno
Was right or not, it might be better to fall silent
And lose ourselves in the curved energy.

We know how many men live alone in their twenties,
And how many women are married to the wrong person,
And how many fathers and sons are strangers to each other.

It's all right if we keep forgetting the way home.
It's all right if we don't remember when we were born.
It's all right if we write the same poem over and over.

Robert, I don't know why you talk so confidently
About yourself in this way. There are a lot of shady
Characters in this town, and you are one of them.

CD: That self-deprecation goes a long way, you know. You seem to be doing that more and more.

RB: Self-deprecation?

CD: Writing that way about yourself.

RB: Good.

CD: Do you remember these lines some time ago? "Why do I suddenly feel free of panic? Here, a summer afternoon, wind-blown lake, a cabin of strong logs. I can live and die with no more fame."

RB: Yes, that was my little cabin up north.

CD: There's another little poem in there that's good too.

RB: Which one? The one that begins "If I could reach down near the earth"?

CD: Yes.

RB: “I could take handfuls of darkness.”

CD: Yes.

RB: “The darkness was always there, which we never noticed.”

Ruth Bly: Why don’t you read one more of the new ones, and then we’ll go have some lunch.

RB: A new one?

CD: Yes. The new ones are terrific.

RB: This is “Keeping Our Small Boat Afloat.”

So many blessings have been given to us
During the first distribution of light, that we are
Admired in a thousand galaxies for our grief.

Don’t expect us to appreciate creation or to
Avoid mistakes. Each of us is a latecomer
To the earth, picking up wood for the fire.

Every night another beam of light slips out
From the oyster’s closed eye. So don’t give up hope
That the door of mercy may still be open.

Seth and Shem, tell me, are you still grieving
Over the spark of light that descended with no
Defender near into the Egypt of Mary’s womb?

It's hard to grasp how much generosity
Is involved in letting us go on breathing,
When we contribute nothing valuable but our grief.

Each of us deserves to be forgiven, if only for
Our persistence in keeping our small boat afloat
When so many have gone down in the storm.

CD: Beautiful.

RB: So that's what it feels like to be 70 or 80 or whatever it is. Each of us deserves to be forgiven. If only for "our persistence in keeping our small boat afloat, when so many have gone down in the storm."

CD: And especially after all you've lived through, the war and the depression.

RB: Yes, and Jim Wright dying.

CD: Yes.

RB: Here's another new poem.

I guess it's an old family
Thing. Someone is Napoleon,
Someone is sacrificed. Call in
Jesus, if you don't get it.

Pick up that cookie on the floor.
Let the hired man go on
Wasting his life. He'll find
Someone to waste it with.

It's like a game in which
The game itself loses.
It's like a picnic in which
The basket eats the food.

It's all right if I go to college;
Most people don't. It's all right
To end up bringing your own
Father home. Just be quiet.

Some powers are stronger
Than we are. They never say
When the battle is.
It was last night. You lost.

CD: These new poems leap with both pathos and humor, as if you'd been waiting your whole life to write these.

RB: Maybe. This one is about my father.

He always knew where he had been, and he remembered
The box elder in the fence post, looked down on men
Who couldn't see the storm coming. He'd learned
To live with the way his bait went deeper.

My mother kept her spirits high with little jobs.
He bought her a heart-shaped box of chocolates
Once a year. One life, one woman,
That was God's rule, and he didn't like it much.

CD: (Laughing) He didn't like it much?

RB: (Laughing) He didn't like it much, no. It tells you how he lived. "He bought her a heart-shaped box of chocolates once a year."

CD: Yeah.

RB: "One life, one woman, that was God's rule, and he didn't like it much."

I don't know how to say it.
We were bumblers—nothing
Was ever clear. Why the war
Started . . . or why the car didn't . . .

We couldn't do it. Probably
Some people understood, but
We just got on the tractor.
We had no one to call meetings.

"Why do you drink?" No one
Asked that, except my mother. She
Did, and the rest of us said, "I don't
Want to be on her side."

CD: These have great wit and wisdom.

RB: (Laughing) "I don't want to be on her side."

Ruth Bly: Well, let's go to lunch.

LUCILLE CLIFTON

About once a month throughout the fall of 2009 I called Lucille Clifton to make arrangements for an interview. I had called several other Cliftons in the Baltimore area in the process of trying to track down the poet Lucille Clifton, unsure if she had a listed number. When she answered the phone on my sixth or seventh try, I knew without knowing her voice that I had finally reached her. "Is this Lucille Clifton, the poet?" I asked. " Tryin' to be," she answered. I explained that I was working on a series of interviews with senior American poets and wanted to include her in this series. She agreed to my request, but asked to see a sampling of my previous interviews, which I sent her that day. When I didn't hear back from her, I called again about a month later. She informed me that she hadn't received my interviews. Her voice seemed more frail. When I called her a third time at the end of November, she commented on how much she had enjoyed reading her old friends' (Maxine Kumin, Galway Kinnell and Ruth Stone) comments about their poetry and lives and agreed to meet with me after Christmas. She then commented that she hadn't been that well lately but would do the best she could. I sensed she was warning me she might not be strong enough to carry through with an interview, but was willing to try. I called her a fourth time after Christmas to set up a specific time and found her still frail but upbeat. She suggested several dates before committing to January 12th, the day before her scheduled cataract procedure.

I traveled from my home in Vermont by train to the Baltimore station, rereading her books and preparing questions. The eight-hour trip passed amazingly quickly. When I arrived on Lucille's doorstep in Columbia, Maryland, she greeted me warmly and invited me in to her attractive town house. She walked slowly as she led me into her living room, then sat in her favorite easy chair by a window. I sat on an adjoining couch and set up my tape recorder on the coffee table in front of us. As soon as we began to talk, I was struck by a remarkable quality in her demeanor: while her physical energy appeared all but enervated, her voice, though weak and barely audible at times, emanated a quiet but indefatigable strength and stamina. Lucille talked for the next three hours without stopping, at one point getting up to show me pictures of her family on the dining room table. By the end of the interview I was exhausted, but Lucille appeared as if she could still go on. She walked me halfway to the front door and wished me well. When I looked back to say goodbye, she was resting against the back of the couch in which I had been sitting, smiling. Three weeks after this interview took place, Lucille Clifton passed away on the same day her mother died in 1959.

CD: Thank you for meeting with me today, Lucille. There's so much I'd like to talk about, I'm not sure where to begin exactly so I'd like to jump around a bit if that's all right with you.

LC: My mind jumps around.

CD: Mine too.

LC: It reminds me of a time I was not feeling well years back and they wanted to figure out whether I was losing my mind, or something like that. They told me I was saying odd things.

CD: But you've been saying odd things your whole life!

LC: (laughing) And they said, "How would we know!"

CD: You've been a vatic poet throughout your career, and vatic poets say odd things.

LC: Oh, people have said that.

CD: Your poems are grounded in truth-telling, colloquial speech, irony, humor, and witness. They emanate what Ruth Stone calls "natural singing." Like Ruth, an old friend of yours, you have, as an outlier, become a celebrated poet within and outside the Academy. In 1999 you were elected to the Board of Chancellors of the Academy of American Poets.

LC: I think it's interesting I'm there.

CD: Soren Kierkegaard wrote that purity of heart is to will one thing. In your poem, "gloria mundi" you write the following: " To serve only one calling, one commitment, one devotion, in one life." This line stresses a powerful singular commitment, yet it's a complex commitment because you've written as an African American woman, as the voice of your slave ancestors, as a mother, as a civil rights worker, as wife, as a children's author and as medium. You sum up all of these voices when you say, "I am a poet." You seem to think that one word, poet, sums up who you are both professionally and personally.

LC: I think it does. I think if someone were to ask me, all of these words would apply. But how does one call herself a pure poet for poetry's sake, when you're going according to some rule not made by poetry, but decided by critics? It changes as critics change. I don't know why. It's not that I don't know some of the rules.

CD: You've always thought of yourself as a craftswoman.

LC: I try to be. I'm a carpenter.

CD: You're a carpenter! Absolutely.

LC: But I do carpentry that is needed for what's going on, in the carpenter's rule, not the poet's rule. One hopes to come ever closer to what poetry wants, what that poem wants.

CD: So the house you're building is your house, but it's a house that is open to your readers.

LC: And they're invited in.

CD: I feel welcome and enlightened in your house of poetry.

LC: I have two sons-in-law who are white and they or other people might think that those are guys I try to be quiet around. Why should I? I'm their mother-in-law you know. I don't try to be quiet in front of anybody about things. They're as human as I am—the same fears, the same hurts.

CD: The word human comes up often in your poetry. When someone resists being human, whether he or she is white, African American or Chinese, you call them on it.

LC: I've noticed that what they're doing is what they would not wish done to them.

CD: In your poem "to ms. ann" you write, "You never called me sister/ then, you never called me sister/ and it has only been forever and/ I will have to forget your face."

LC: Yes.

CD: Throughout your work there is a constant public struggle that parallels the private struggles of your life.

LC: And they have been many!

CD: You have experienced great loss, great suffering, and yet, like Job's messenger, here you still are, reporting the news of your struggles. Yet despite the social, economic and racial oppression you've chronicled from both a personal and political perspective, you continually find reason to hope and thrive.

LC: That's interesting.

CD: In poems such as " good friday," "the making of poems," "hag riding," "roots," "memory," "spring song" and "blessing the boats"—all these poems end with such stalwart affirmation. I'm wondering if this hope and strength in you, which emanate from family, faith and poetry come from any other place or are simply a reflection of who you are.

LC: I don't think my children think of me as a particularly strong woman. No, they do think of me as a strong woman, but not perhaps as a hopeful one. I know that miracles happen. I know that. You know, we think of a miracle as something or other, but a miracle can be a very tiny thing.

CD: Yes.

LC: I'm not as strong as I used to be. I'm 73, of course now. But in my head, I think of myself as a super woman.

CD: I know you do. In your poem "hag riding" you write: "why/ is what i ask myself/ maybe it is the African in me/ still trying to get home/ after all these years/ but when I wake to the heat of morning/ galloping down the highway of my life/ something hopeful rises in me/ rises and runs me out into the road/ and i lob my fierce thigh high/ into the rump of the day and honey/ i ride i ride"

LC: "Honey, I ride." That's fun. I mean it's what happens.

CD: Yes.

LC: And why does it happen? I can't begin to know why. But I'm not supposed to know why. Why do I deserve such wonderfulness?

CD: Many of your poems are about witnessing to horrible events.

LC: And feeling them.

CD: Which is what your children pick up on.

LC: Yeah, I guess so.

CD: Feeling them deeply, and writing about them.

LC: Yeah, witnessing. I think that's an important thing with regard to what we do.

CD: You specifically state your role as a witness in your poem “monday sundown 9/17/01” from your most recent book mercy: “i bear witness to no thing/ more human than hate// i bear witness to no thing/ more human than love// apples and honey/ apples and honey/ what is not lost/ is paradise”

LC: That was written during Chanukah, I think. My daughter’s clients are mostly orthodox. I’ve always been part of that tradition.

CD: You’ve written a lot about Old and New Testament figures, especially in your book some jesus, as well as about the Hindu goddess Cali.

LC: Yes.

CD: And also Milton’s Lucifer, whom you view as your alter ego as a “light bringer” like yourself, “created out of fire” to illuminate, which, as you write in “lucifer speaks in his own voice,” you have done as Lucille, the female light bearer.

LC: Yes.

CD: Even though you might not point to one religion and say, “That’s what I am,” you possess a strong spiritual core that draws eclectically on a wide range of religious traditions.

LC: I don’t go to church at all.

CD: You have written many poems that aren’t religious per se, but are devotional or prayerful.

LC: I know that sort of thing.

CD: You were raised a Southern Baptist.

LC: Yes. I remember the first day I didn't want to go to church. I said, "Daddy, I don't think I want to go to church today." And it was like death! The avenging daddy!

CD: What happened?

LC: No. I lay there guilty all morning.

CD: Did you go next week?

LC: I probably did. I don't remember.

CD: This is characteristic of you.

LC: Really?

CD: You reject institutions.

LC: That's probably it, yes.

CD: You attended Howard University from 1953 to 1954 as a drama major.

LC: I had to leave; I didn't have any money.

CD: But didn't you decide that you didn't want to stay? You've said you lost your scholarship because you didn't study.

LC: I thought I was smart. Each year I learn how not smart I am.

CD. You had some remarkable fellow students—Amiri Barak, Toni Morrison, Roberta Flak.

LC: Didn't I!

CD: Amazing.

LC: I've known Amiri Baraka all my adult life.

CD: You studied with Sterling Brown, Owen Dodson and James Baldwin who assisted Dodson in directing his play, *The Amen Corner*, which you were in.

LC. Yes.

CD: You knew if you didn't study you would lose your scholarship.

LC: Yes.

CD: You then went to Fredonia in Buffalo for a short while, but didn't graduate. You met your husband Fred through Ishmael Reed and got married in 1958, then went to work as a claims supervisor in the Buffalo unemployment office for two years before getting pregnant with your first child, Sydney.

LC: Yes.

CD: One baby after another came after Sydney.

LC: (laughing) That was my job! And I was faithful to my job.

CD: You had six children—Sydney, Fredrica, Channing, Gillian, Graham, and Alexia— between 1959 and 1965.

LC: Yes. The last three were less than two years apart.

CD: Amazing.

LC: I think so too!

C: What a strong woman!

LC: I had never even been around babies.

CD: You must have been writing throughout the sixties somehow because in 1966 Langston Hughes included several of your poems in his anthology *The Poetry of the Negro, 1746-1970.* He died in 1967, but the anthology appeared in 1970.

LD: Yes.

CD: He loved your work.

LC: He really did. I had a letter from him.

CD: And then Random House accepted your book *good times* in 1969. During the tumultuous sixties when you were raising your children, you were somehow writing poetry on the side.

LC: Yes, and Toni Morrison was my editor.

CD: And that book launched your career.

LC: I don't know why. I was shocked that anybody wanted to read it. Toni's inclination was to put things in and mine was to take things out.

CD: Did she succeed in convincing you to put more poems in?

LC: I'm fairly meek about some things, but not my work. Nobody messes with my work.

CD: So you prevailed?

LC: I'm scared of Toni now. There are two people I am in awe of, and Toni's one. The other is Adrianne Rich, who doesn't know I'm in awe of her.

CD: But you knew her very well, right?

LC: Yes. When we both lived in Santa Cruz, our children both had some disease, I forget. Anyway, we were worried about our children.

CD: You have lost two children within the last eight years.

LC: Yes.

CD: Channing…

LC: Yes, Channing…my little son.

CD: I'm sorry. And your daughter Fredrica?

LC: She had a brain tumor like Fred. I thought we'd all be together forever, but…

CD: In your poem, "wild blessings" you write "i'm grateful for many blessings/ but the gift of understanding,/ the wild one, maybe not." So when you say "the understanding," do you mean the understanding of suffering, the comprehension of suffering.

LC: Yes. Because it's not always a blessing, you know.

CD: I know.

LC: To understand is to not condemn, first of all. It's almost an excuse for feeling sorry for yourself too, and for feeling proud of how noble you are and that sort of thing. And then my family, because my mother died at forty four; my father was forty nine, as was my husband, Fred, when he died. Channing and Fredrica died in their thirties. I'm the oldest living person in my family, and I'm young, you know. I'm not old.

CD: Alexia, your youngest daughter, has given back to you.

L: Alexia has taken care of me in a lot of ways.

CD: She donated a kidney to you, right?

LC: Yes, and when I was feeling so sick, she would say, "People don't give you their organs so you can complain about it." She's a tough little something…quite a lot like her father.

CD: I see. So you were surprised when your first book *good times* took off.

LC: I was very embarrassed.

CD: Why?

LC: It was like, what I said had anything to do with anything. You know what I mean?

CD: You were then suddenly thrust into the limelight with *good times* with Langston Hughes calling you an important, new voice in American poetry. That must have been such a heady time for you.

LC: Well, I haven't got a grip on it yet. Because the idea that I might matter…I mean, everybody matters, you know. I'm conflicted about it.

CD: And your success continued. Many of your books were finalists for the Pulitzer Prize and you won the National Book Award in 2000 for *blessing the boats*.

LC: Yes.

CD: You've become a celebrated American poet. In fact, you're the only poet ever to have two books—*next* and *good woman*—chosen as finalists for the Pulitzer Prize in the same year.

LC: Yes. Well there's a way you're supposed to look if you're an American poet. There's a way you're supposed to sound.

CD: And what do you think of that?

LC: I think it's hogwash you know.

CD: You go back and forth between being “an ordinary woman” and an extraordinary woman. Don’t you think?

LC: I guess so. (laughing). My family always encouraged me to do what I wanted to. I’m from Dahomey women.

CD: But in your own mind there’s an ongoing dialectic at play between your identity as ordinary, as your book *ordinary woman* emphasizes, and your simultaneous view of yourself as extraordinary, even mystical, someone who receives, as we see in your book the ones who talk in which you transcribe your dead mother’s prophetic warnings about “the fate and dangers of the world of the Americas.”

LC: Yes, that’s true. I think that’s important.

CD: What do you think Langston Hughes saw in your early poems?

LC: I have no idea! He was nice, nice man, as I try to be a nice person.

CD: I think he saw your irony.

LC: Well I have a lot of humor and I see humor in a lot of stuff.

CD: Humor with bite and wit. The poems Langston Hughes anthologized in *Poetry of the Negro*, poems that also appeared in your first book *good times*, alternate between the kind of ironic witness that was typical of slave songs, songs slaves sang within earshot of their masters about their oppression and plight but in a way their tone deaf masters couldn’t grasp, and plain-speaking laments and celebrations. I’m thinking in particular of such poems as "in the inner city" in the first category and "robert" and "good times" in the second.

LC: Yes. My father used to sing for us songs that the slaves sang. His side of the family came to this country in 1830.

CD: Right. Is that that when Caroline, your great grandmother the midwife, walked from New Orleans to Bedford, Virginia?

LC: Yes. And they went to a plantation, Mr. Sayle's plantation.

CD: In Bedford County.

LC: I've been to that. I got into Bedford, Ca'line and I, Cal… and when (heavy breath) we got there, when they got there. You notice that?

CD: You were there weren't you?

LC: I don't know. Alls I know is that…I'll tell you that ground is very familiar to me. I met a woman in the library in Bedford.

CD: I've been there.

LC: Really?

CD: Yes. I grew up in Bedford County, just down the road from Bedford Lake, Big Island and Natural Bridge.

LC: Oh, I've heard of those places.

CD: Your father said he changed your name from Sayle to Sayles because he wanted there to be many of you, right?

LC: He wanted there to be a lot of him. He called me Lucilleman. He always called me Lucille and the man, Lucilleman. Why, I have no clue! And my brother, he wasn't him.

CD: You wrote a sad elegy for him.

LC: Oh I loved him so much and his children…he wasn't married, but he, with the same woman, they might as well have been married.

CD: Your father had a child from his first marriage.

LC: That's Jo.

CD: That's Jo and her mother died when she was very young of TB.

LC: Probably. There was a lot of that around.

CD: Then he married your mother, Thelma.

LC: Ma said that he promised if she'd marry him, he'd buy her all new clothes. So she said, "Hell!." (laughing) She said that one Christmas, he said if she married him, he'd give her clothes and she said, "And I never got my clothes!"

CD: Oh no! And then you were born.

LC: I came along and then Elaine who is six months younger than I am. It's funny because on her birthday I call her and say, "You're my age, ha ha ha."

CD: She's the daughter of the woman who was a friend of your father and your mother.

LC: Right. And my aunt, my mother's younger sister, she was her best friend. And at some point, my mother…my mother always said that you don't blame children for the adult's mistake. So we grew up six months apart from each other.

CD: You feel like she's your closest sister.

LC: Yes, and anybody could be my sister.

CD: Anybody could be your sister?

LC: You know, I mean, the best kind of thing. As black people, we don't know who our sisters are. We have as much right as anybody to call each other sisters.

CD: A section of your book *an ordinary woman* is titled "sisters." You make an observation about family in your memoir *generations* that is pertinent along these lines. "When the colored people came to Depew they came to be a family. Everybody began to be related in thin ways that last and last. The generations of white folks are just people but the generations of colored folks are families."

LC: Yes, and that would be natural wouldn't it? Because those families have been torn up. I think it's interesting that white people enter that family thing. I've got a lot of friends. My best friend is white, and she's wonderful. She's Catholic, married to a Jew! They're kids are little militants of all sorts. And then I have another friend who's Hindu, whose husband was Sikh. They're almost worlds apart. I seem to attract diversity!

CD: Again in *generations*, you write, "Love rejected hurts so much more than love rejecting. They act like they don't love their country. No, what it is, is that they find out that their country don't love them." This reminded me of a remark Michelle Obama's made during the 2008 campaign, for which she received a lot of criticism from white conservatives. Her precise words were: "For the first time in my adult lifetime, I'm really proud of my country, and not just because Barack has done well, but because I think people are hungry for change."

LC: Well I'm proud of the remark she made.

CD: How could anyone not understand her sentiment in light of this country's racial history?

LC: Because they don't dare understand what she was talking about. How dare she not be grateful?

CD: You come from a long line of strong women.

LC: My father used to always say we're from a family of strong women and weak men.

CD: Well the Dahomey women are from a tribe of warrior women.

LC: Yes. There's another Dahomey woman who is well known, and that's Audrey Lord. She is a Dahomey woman.

CD: I have a Nigerian colleague, E.C. Osondu, who is a fiction writer and this year's winner of the Caine Prize who prepared this question for you. "Lucille has traced her ancestry to Dahomey in West Africa, where there is a tradition of strong female warriors. Does she see herself in the mold of the female warriors of poetry? What is her attitude toward awards, accolades, prizes, recognitions for poets? What is she putting in place to give the poetry world many more Lucille Cliftons?"

LC: I don't think that much of prizes and awards. I mean they are fine, and one is proud, but you can't take it that seriously. Who can say she's this kind when she's this kind? This is all superfluous to me.

CD: Your prizes and awards, which have been numerous don't seem to have affected your poetry.

LC: This is not public yet, so we won't say it right away. But this year, I won the Robert Frost Prize from the Poetry Society of America.

CD: Congratulations! Well deserved.

LC: Thank you.

CD: Do you plan on attending the annual Poetry Society of America prize ceremony?

LC: Yes. "So, get well," the girls say, because I can't be walking funny.

CD: You'll do fine, I'm sure. You're going to get that cataract fixed tomorrow, just like that other one. So it's nice to get these awards?

LC: It's nice. You go to New York and see friends you don't see all the time.

CD: And you'll read a poem or two?

LC: I've got to write one! The girls keep saying, "Be quiet, let her write! Write, Mom!" You know, write? Okay! I'm the worst person in the world for that. Doing assignments just isn't what I do.

CD: So you've won an award from the Poetry Society of America named after a famous New England poet who never, to my knowledge, wrote one poem about an African American.

LC: Isn't that wild! It's funny. When I was a Chancellor at the Academy of American Poets we put Gwen Brooks' name up for the Frost prize, and it took five or six ballots.

CD: What?

LC: I don't understand why. Gwen Brooks is so important to poetry.

CD: You are both known for your powerful vernacular voices.

LC: Yes.

CD: There's a wonderful stanza from your sectional poem "heroes" in your book *good news* about the earth where you address the ironic efficacy of the vernacular as that spoken, colloquial expression of the crazy man who turns "nigger into prince." You write, "i am high on the man called crazy/ who has turned nigger into prince/ and broken his words on every ear./ he is blinded by the truth/ his nose is sharp with courage./ this crazy man has given his own teeth/ to eat devils and out of mine/ he has bitten suns."

LC: I like that.

CD: The line I keep going back to is: "and broken his words on every ear." It's that unabashed vernacular Langston Hughes insisted on throughout his career, and also Gwendolyn Brooks, that breaks the ear—language that is subversive, rebellious, ungrammatical, direct, musical, spoken.

LC: I hope so.

CD: It resonates language that breaks the ear as opposed to coddling the ear with embellishment and decoration.

LC: Yeah, those things are not friends of poetry I don't think–embellishment. Things don't need that. If you have the right language, if you just get the correct…not only what the language means in the dictionary, but the sound. Word's have sound and music. It's the difference between pretty and beautiful. I used to tell my students that pretty people want to be beautiful, but beautiful people aren't trying to get pretty. You need to feel the language. There is a language that one chooses because it chooses itself almost.

CD: Your language seems to choose itself, that is, come to you. It's almost as if you're transcribing your poems.

LC: Absolutely.

CD: There's a wonderful example of this in *good times*, in a poem about the yearly strikes your father participated in at the steel mill where he worked in Buffalo. The language in this poem is so oral yet it makes its way to the page at the same time as memorable poetic expression.

chipping like hell
on eight days and off one
sleeping rights between the rows of couplers
hard and stinking out across the field
through the polack picket line
and the strike was broke

lord, child I love the union

worked together
slept
fought
in the same town
all the pork chops
fired hard together
stinking together
oh mammy ca'line

a nigger polack ain't shit
now my first wife never did come out of her room
until her shoes was buttoned

mamma looked at me and said"
you always was a bad boy

and died
gould train come through and
i got on

grandpaw's girls was young
could write
their old timey friend was pregnant
and they said they'd pay my bills
the man was gone
and she was clean as mama

was a girl

never came out of her room
until her shoes was buttoned
scrubbed the walls sometimes
twice a day
and I would make her stop   clean
till she died
twenty-one years old
so was granpaw's girl
your mama
i like to marry friends

LC: That's my father.

CD: There's that language breaking the ear, a passionate, oral language that's ancient and at the same time modern and timeless.

LC: Well I used to worry about that. I didn't write in that way because I didn't know it. I didn't study it. All of this language, we all are speaking our second language. This isn't Britain, although, we like to think it is. I don't know. The Inuit don't speak like the Eskimos. We in this country seem to feel that we are starting to become diverse. For heaven's sake, what does that mean? I find it fascinating. We talk all different kinds of ways. And there are a lot of different ones speaking Western English and Eastern English. And yet, on the one hand they are all different, and on the other hand… I'm thinking ahead of myself. If you go to a lot of different places, and you look at television, or listen to the radio, there's only one English that is accepted as valid English. That's the English along the Eastern seaboard. Young people are always trying to get a language together so they have their own thing, you know? It's natural. Now it's so Spanish influenced…as my son-in-law tells me. I have one daughter who's not married, my baby, Alexia.

CD: Does she want to get married?

LC: Oh, you know, she's at peace with it. She probably does, but she's at peace. And I know she ought to get married and hopefully she will. I hope so, because she'd be such a good mother. And you don't have to be married to be a good mother, of course not but…I'm aware of being in the way a little bit for that.

CD: Well, I could just tell from the tone of her voice the other day on the phone how much she loves you and enjoys taking care of you.

LC: Well she's my mother actually!

CD: She's your mother?

LC: I don't tell anybody. Would you like to see some photographs?

CD: I'd love to. (Lucille led me to a table in her dining room that displayed standing pictures of her children, grandchildren, late husband and children-in-law. In describing the picture of late husband, Fred, running in the New York City marathon, she commented, "He was pretty sure he was the model God was aiming for.")

CD: Thank you for showing me these pictures of your family. I notice you don't have any pictures of you mother here.

LC: I do, but they're upstairs.

CD: You include a picture of her in your memoir *Generations*.

LC: She was forty when she died and my father was forty nine, and now I'm old and crotchety.

CD: You think you're crotchety?

LC: I'm impatient about things more than anything else. The person I've known the longest in connection to my family is Ishmael Reed. We grew up together.

CD: He introduced you to Fred, didn't he?

LC: Yes.

CD: He recently retired from Berkeley where he taught for over three decades, but he grew up with you in Buffalo.

LC: I knew the Reeds, his mother and brother. His mother's name is Thelma. My original name is Thelma. My full name is Thelma Lucille.

CD: Do you remember when you decided to take the name Lucille?

LC: Well, that was my middle name. They wanted to name me Georgia, because my father's mother's name was Georgia. She was crotchety, my grandmother. I think she was a nut, very crotchety. Boy, she was crotchety. My father said she was the meanest woman he ever knew.

CD: Did you know her?

LC: Yeah. I thought she was crazy. But so are a lot of people!

CD: She had probably been through a whole lot. Your mother was epileptic later in her life.

LD: Yes. I'd listen at night to be sure that if she had a seizure, somebody could go and see about it.

CD: You have a sweet poem that's dedicated to her in your book *mercy* titled "o antic god." Do you recall it?

LC: I'm not sure.

CD: It goes like this:

oh my antic God
return to me
my mother in her thirties

leaned across the front porch
the huge pillow of her breasts
pressing against the rail
summoning me in for bed.

i'm almost a dead woman's age times two.
i can barely recall her song
the scent of her hands
though her wild hair scratches my dreams
at night. return to me, oh Lord of then
and now, my mother's calling,
her young voice humming my name.

LD: Oh, that is a nice one.

CD: Isn't that beautiful?

LC: She was like that, amazingly knowledgeable.

CD: Forty years before you wrote that poem, you wrote these lines about your mother.

My momma moved among the days
like a dream walker in a field;
seemed like what she touched was hers
seemed like what touched her couldn't hold
she got us almost through the high grass
then seemed like she turned around and ran
right back in
right back on in

There is a bitter-sweetness in this earlier poem from *good times.*

LC: Yes.

CD: You were probably wishing just after having six children yourself that she had been around.

LC: I hoped.

CD: You must have missed her terribly.

LC: Oh, my! We were sitting up on New Year's Eve. We had a piano, which was unusual, and I would sit there trying to play on New Year's Eve. I've never had a New Years Eve when I didn't cry.

CD: Did she die on New Year's Eve?

LC: No. It was February, Friday the 13th whatever year. [Lucille herself died on this day in 2010, three weeks after this interview.]

CD: It was 1959. But there was something about…

LC: Something about another year she's not going to be…she's not coming back. While it's the beginning of a lot of stuff—New Years' Eve—it's not the beginning for others.

CD: When you started hearing her voice, receiving those poems in the ones who talk, what was that like for you, because it was…your mother with whom you were communicating?

LC: You hesitated to say it was my mother.

CD: I did.

LC: But it was my mother.

CD: It was your mother.

LC: Because I, I mean, I grew up in the Baptist Church, Southern Baptist. My mother was sanctified, which is a little more than…

CD: Than baptized?

LC: Than Baptist, yes, but it's hard to understand.

CD: Sort of like, maybe, what the Catholics do with saints?

LC: Maybe. But I think the Catholics can be extreme. When I was young, I always thought there was more than this. I mean, why would there only be this? You know, why?

CD: When you say "this", you mean this world?

LC: This world as we manifest it.

CD: You had this feeling from a young age?

LC: Yes, that this wasn't all.

CD: And so this communication with your mother happened in the '70s?

LC: We had a Ouija board, and we started, the girls…my two oldest girls, Sydney and Fredrica, and I, and Rica would take down this Ouija board and that just happened. I remember that quite well. It was raining and we were in Buffalo and we wanted to go to the movies and it was too rainy to go to the movies, and so, Sydney—we always had a lot of games and a lot of game playing in the family—got out the things for games, and Rica said something like, "Look at this, it's a Ouija board, let's look at it." And then, Syd and I started touching it and all of a sudden it jumps. My kids and I thought anything could happen with me, and Syd said, "Stop, Ma. Stop it. Don't do this." And I said, "I'm not doing anything."

CD: You weren't doing anything?

LC: I'm not doing anything, and I don't want to do anything!

CD: But it was going?

LC: Yes, and it started moving, and it was tough. I started saying, "Who? Sydney, this is not funny. So it started spelling out, you know.

CD: And who was writing down the words?

LC: Fredrica. She was translating and transcribing, and Syd and I were holding. It started spelling out, and Frederica was getting scared, saying, "Who's doing this? I want to stop!" And it just whizzed and spelled "Thelma." Yes. Thelma, and then it dashed off, "Now rest, go to bed, we'll talk later." And we had sense enough to...

CD: To obey it?

LC: Yes.

CD: Did it start with the teapot poem that begins “your mother sends you this// you have a teapot/ others have teapots/ if you abuse them/ they will break.”

LC: Yes. They were explaining, “you have a teapot, others have a teapot.” You treat them right, they will, you know…You have a gift, others have a gift.

CD: Was it spelling this out?

LC: It was writing with her hand and then Syd started writing. So you had to go back through it and see what the words were.

CD: Was anything coming to you? Did it come to your hand?

LC: It was my hand after a while, after a little while. And I knew that this was odd and the girls, they had a right to say, “No way. I’m not doing that anymore.”

CD: Yeah. But they kept on.

LC: They kept on for a while, for a bit.

CD: And then it was just you?

LC: And then it was just me writing.

CD: How did you know your communication with Thelma was over?

LC: It was over. You could just feel it.

CD: A departure?

LC: A lifting.

CD: You were born with six fingers, but I can't see where they were now.

LC: There and there. Somebody told me I have hands that look like I have never worked. And I've had a job since I was twelve. Somebody asked me also…people have often asked me what it's metaphor for. And I said, it's not metaphor for anything. I was born with twelve fingers. Yeah, I don't do metaphor.

CD: You write a lot about you're the six fingers you were born with on each hand. I think your poem "speaking of loss" from *good woman* is my favorite on this subject. "i began with everything;/ parents, two extra fingers/ a brother to ruin. i was a rich/ girl with no money/ in a red dress./ how did I come/ to sit in this house/ wearing a name I'd never heard/ until I was a woman? someone has stolen/ my parents, and hidden my brother./ my extra fingers are cut away./ I am left with plain hands and/ nothing to give you but poems."

LC: I think that's true.

CD: So in a way, your missing fingers are metaphorical in this poem in that they endow you with a invaluable "plainness." It is the absence of those fingers that spawn your poems. As the result of losing both the outward sign of your extraordinariness and your parents and brother you wrote poems that convert your losses into poetry.

LC: Yeah. It's interesting.

CD: The fact that you were born with six fingers, along with being a Dahomey woman, makes you quite extraordinary as "an ordinary woman."

LC: (laughing) I am an extraordinary woman. There is an African tradition of women who have some extra thing, you know?

CD: Chinua Achebe writes a lot about the Yoruba folklore of extra things in *Things Fall Apart*. Twins are considered particularly mystical, even demonic.

LC: And do you know that I have always been interested in twins? Why just the thought of twins and people who are twins but not twins, if you can figure out what I mean.

CD: Oh yes. It's interesting what you said about Alexia and your mother, how people inhabit other people sometimes. I was just looking for your poem about the ordinary women. You end that poem by saying, "i had expected to be more than this./ i had not expected to be/an ordinary woman."

LC: Yes.

CD: Yet at the time you wrote that, you must have known that you were more than ordinary.

LC: Or at least I paid attention. I had to tell students all the time that the thing we had to do in order to write well is first of all be true to it. I know what people want me to write.

CD: What do you think people want you to write?

LC: I'm the noble, nice one. I was born a week before June Jordon.

CD: You were?

LC: Yeah. And I'm supposed to write about suffering. I don't think I suffer more than anybody else. I think that people don't acknowledge…because we think it's inhuman to suffer or to have hard times. We think that the gods are supposed to pay specific attention to us. And I've had miracles that I don't think I'm…I know I'm not the only person to have miracles, but I know that we all have had a miracle of some kind. And I'm a believer in reincarnation. I don't know any other way to explain my poetry, that I do write it and that I wish to write it.

CD: Well something that keeps coming through your poetry is your enormous affirmation that offsets a lot of the witnessing of horrible things. You're like Anne Frank in the attic saying, "Despite everything, I believe that people are really good at heart," when she had no reason to say this in the midst of Nazi occupation.

LC: It's like we're not seeing this the right way, we're not looking at this lined up as it could also be. It's either that or perhaps it's this. And one should leave room for the "perhaps." I think it was barbarous the time that the plane bombed the tent in which Khadafi's son was sleeping. That was terrible. That's not oh well, we had to do it. No we didn't. I don't know what the alternative is, because I can't think that way. My mind isn't like that. But my mind does like to keep an opening for possibility.

CD: Along these lines, you wrote a poem to the Black Panthers titled “apology.” It’s in *good news about the earth.*

LC: Oh, right.

CD: I’d like to read it to you.

i became a woman
during the old prayers
among the ones who wore
bleaching cream to bed
and all my lessons stayed

i was obedient
but brothers I thank you
for these mannish days

i remember again the wise one
old and telling of suicides
refusing to be slaves

i had forgotten and
brothers I thank you
i praise you
i grieve my whiteful ways

You tread a fine line here between accepting the Black Panthers “mannish ways” and remaining prayerful, preserving the lessons that “stayed.”

LC: I was a happy little housewife, and I felt free to be so. I liked the sort of people who were foolish. None of us is the princess or prince of black poetry.

CD: It gets back to what you keep saying about being a poet, which encompasses many identities for you, as opposed to being the princess of black poetry.

LC: Well, I wouldn't even want to do that. Why would I want to do that? Why would I even want to? Just to express something as one of the witnesses of that, and there's more than one. There's always more than one.

CD: I'm moved by both the particular and the universal in your work that safeguards it from becoming two dimensional.

LC: How do I do it for my students? It's not like the general can show you the specific. The specific can show you the general. So trying to say to students, that's…write about love. How do you know? That's how I feel about Hershey's with almonds.

CD: Did you read any women poets when you first started to write?

LC: Other than Gwen Brooks, I can't think of anyone.

CD: She was quite a bit older than you.

LC: Pretty much, about twenty years, but we became friends.

CD: She was a mentor?

LC: No, but she was a friend. I don't think I've had people ask me, I can't recall anyone who was a mentor because I wasn't around them. I was in Buffalo. Buffalo's a Polish town.

CD: The struggle of love of love that abides in your work, I see it in your elegies. I see it in your relationship with your mother and father. They were hard times, extremely hard, yet you write about them affectionately. There's no grudge there. I know you could have held a grudge very easily against your father.

LC: Oh, absolutely. I could have hated him…thought I would at one time.

CD: You show a selfless love, especially when you talk about him in heaven.

LC : (laughing) It never occurred to me.

CD: This is what I meant at the start of the interview when I said there was a prophetic or vatic quality to your poetry that transcends poetry for poetry's sake, or poetry for politics' sake, and that's just who you are, I think.

LC: I think so. I think, for some reason, I'm just this way. I have no idea why. It's nice, but I mean…

CD: It doesn't make you soft.

LC: No, I don't think I am. I'm tough. What good does it do to not be if I can see the human in you I can see the human in me, and that's nice.

CD: Well that takes a special vision. You've got these glasses on.

LC: I'm just taking them off, and it's so weird, because now I see double, quite often. I hope that's going to be fixed tomorrow.

CD: What do you think of the state of poetry today in this country?

LC: I think that people's expectations are being turned around in many ways because people have always had certain things work because there was a certain kind of expectation. Because we think of things, not only what we're like, but our own stereotypes of things, you know?

CD: But what do you think about the huge tent of American poetry? You came up before the Internet and the proliferation of poetry programs and the AWP.

LC: These things do young, minority poets a disservice because if they don't see each other in some place, they don't know that they can be there. Well, like Squaw Valley, a lot of minority people don't think they can be there. I taught there twenty years ago. I think a lot of minority people don't know that they can be there, and I got there twenty years ago. So you've got to see someone else somewhere.

CD: Are you associated with Cave Canem?

LC: I am an elder there.

CD: That's an amazing organization where tremendous young talent has developed.

LC: You have to pay attention to Cave Canem. Some black people together in their own place. Toy Derricotte and Cornelius Eady are remarkable poets and people. I think it's good to see poets who are friends. That's why I enjoy being with Toy and Sharon Olds and Galway Kinnell and reading with them. People have to know that I'm a poet just like Galway is. We know that. But I don't believe in either/or, I believe in both/and. But you might have to have Cave Canem.

CD: There is certainly a lot of very strong, young African American talent that has emerged from Cave Canem in the last several years—such poets as Camille Dungy, Ross Gay, Terrance Hays, Major Jackson, Patricia Smith, Regie O'Hare Gibson and Kevin Young, Tara Betts, Shara McCallum and Harryette Mullen, Natasha Trethewey ,to mention only a few.

LC: Yes. And they tend to be, now, it's almost true…or it could be true, that Washington and Pittsburgh, where Cave Canem is, are centers of black poetry.

CD: How are you feeling?

LC: I'm fine.

CD: You're amazing. We've been talking for almost two hours.

LC: See, I'm a big mouth.

CD: Do you remember what your first job was?

LC: What was my first job? The first job I ever had was watching a little girl. I received one dollar, and my mother made me go and give it back.

CD: Why?

LC: My aunt worked for this lady as a seamstress. She did laundry and my aunt got me the job, and she was able to get me a job watching. The little girl's name was Heather. How odd that I remember her name. I remember I didn't know I was going to be paid, but I was ready to be paid. I watched her every day, five days, and when the time came for her to pay me—I was nice twelve-year-old—and the women gave me, bundled up, the money, and it was a dollar. I knew there were people who got more than that. I didn't know they were twelve. I took it home and said, "Mom, she didn't but give me one dollar!" I had worked five days, from after school until about six. And I said, "Ma, she just gave me one dollar!" I was ready to cry and my mother was mad. I had never seen her furious. And she said, "You take it right back to her, and tell her to buy some toilet paper." This was a biggy, you know. So I went back with the dollar back and said "My momma said use it for toilet paper." Well my mother told me to say that. So I didn't go back to work, but I was crying. And my mother was so angry. And she was too, because I think she knew I was getting something for more than she had paid for. And then the next week I got a job working at a jewelry place and I worked from then on until I left for Howard.

CD: I forgot to just mention your children's books.

LC: Oh I love children's' books. They're not as easy to write as people think.

CD: You also worked with Marlowe Thomas.

LC: Yes. I thought I was hot stuff.

CD: You were.

LC: I know.

CD: You won an Emmy for co-writing the screenplay for Free To Be You And Me.

LC: I went to AWP, as a matter of fact--the first year--and she, Marlowe Thomas, gave a reception, you know, and I remember I tried very hard to be like, "Look at all these white people, everyone!" But I was one of the few black writers there. Of course that's what I saw, that's what I always saw! We used to meet for *Free To Be You And Me* once every couple of weeks, the group that was writing the show. I met some interesting people. I have met more people who are interesting than I ever would have met in my life. To me, my ambition was to get to Kleinhans Music Hall in Buffalo. And I did.

CD: Did you give a reading there?

LC: Yes.

CD: That's great. You've read a number of times in Buffalo?

LC: Not as often as you'd think. I'm going to Eerie Community College next month.

CD: Are you still writing?

LC: That's an odd question, don't you think?

CD: Yeah. It always is. I don't know how to answer it myself.

LC: I'm writing, if I would be so blessed to write something. I haven't written since I've been feeling badly. I've been ill, but it's coming back. I feel it. I don't know why I would stop.

CD: Well I don't either, unless you were forced to in some way. You've been very prolific.

LC: That's what they tell me.

CD: It doesn't seem that way to you?

LC: Not at all. I know how often I don't write. I was in despair or in a depression for some time, but I'm going to be okay.

CD: So your spirits are a little better?

LC: Yeah.

CD: Good. That's good to hear.

LC: The girls were saying, "Mommy, try to be lucid. Try very hard."

CD: Were they worried that you weren't going to be lucid?

LC: I don't know what they thought.

CD: You know, your poems are full of references to madness and craziness.

LC: Probably!

CD: You have a poem called a "poem for the mad" and you love Crazy Horse.

LC: I do!

CD: Do you associate craziness with being a poet at all?

LC: Well, a little bit. Perhaps more than a little bit. Crazy could mean spirited, magical. It could be all these things.

CD: I know in a lot of your poems about craziness, you write about the poet as a kind of fool. You make disclaimers for the poet. In your poem "the poet" you write, " i beg my bones to be good but/ they keep clicking music and/ I spin in the center of myself/ a foolish frightful woman/ moving my skin against the wind and/ tap-dancing for my life."

LC: I like that.

CD: In your poem "admonitions" you write similarly, "children/ when they ask you/ why is your mama so funny/ say she is a poet/ she don't have no sense"

LC: True. My kids probably said that too.

CD: You have this wonderful sense of self-effacing irony and in much of your work the poet is the witness, the truth-teller, the mother, the spokeswoman for lawgivers, which is the term Whitman coined for his fellow citizens. And yet you're calling that person—the poet--a fool at the same time.

LC: There's some truth in that.

CD: What do you think the truth is in that appellation?

LC: I don't know. But there is something that rings true to the ear.

CD: Do you feel poets need to be knocked off their pedestals?

LC: Yes. They often think that they're smarter than everybody else.

CD: Do you believe the poet has to be on the same level as the people in order to speak credibly?

LC: Poets have to speak out of what is truth for them. Everything we say has so many meanings. I'm shy. I'm really quite shy. Nobody believes it.

CD: But you're sane…you've been sane the whole time we've been talking…you've been very sane the whole time we've been talking.

LC: Thank you. To be sane in this world is crazy.

Essays

THE PLACE WHERE YOU LIE: A READING OF JAMES WRIGHT'S "TO THE MUSE"

In thinking about the elusive appeal of enduring love lyrics, I return over and over to the striking contemporary poem "To the Muse" by James Wright, which curiously, given Wright's sustained popularity and critical attention since his death in 1980, has not received, to my knowledge, the kind of close reading it deserves since its publication in *Shall We Gather at the River* in 1968. The speaker, in his address to his beloved, gives voice to a host of extreme emotions and thoughts throughout this poem that range from human unknowing to a progressively changing yet freshly present agony to unbridled intimacy to an unrestrained protest against the sheer impossibility of life to an ultimately illuminating madness. Is there another contemporary love poem that explores the grieving lover's bardo state with commensurate economy, intensity, and sprezzatura?

To The Muse

It is all right. All they do
Is go in by dividing
One rib from another. I wouldn't
Lie to you. It hurts
Like nothing I know. All they do
Is burn their way in with a wire.
It forks in and out a little like the tongue
Of that frightened garter snake we caught
At Cloverfield, you and me, Jenny
So long ago.

I would lie to you
If I could.
But the only way I can get you to come up
Out of the suckhole, the south face

Of the Powhatan pit, is to tell you
What you know:

You come up after dark, you poise alone
With me on the shore.
I lead you back to this world.

Three lady doctors in Wheeling open
Their offices at night.
I don't have to call them, they are always there.
But they only have to put the knife once
Under your breast.
Then they hang their contraption.
And you bear it.

It's awkward a while. Still it lets you
Walk about on tiptoe if you don't
Jiggle the needle.
It might stab your heart, you see.
The blade hangs in your lung and the tube
Keeps it draining.
That way they only have to stab you
Once. Oh Jenny.

I wish to God I had made this world, this scurvy
And disastrous place. I

Didn't, I can't bear it
Either, I don't blame you, sleeping down there
Face down in the unbelievable silk of spring,
Muse of the black sand,

Alone.

I don't blame you, I know
The place where you lie.
I admit everything. But look at me.
How can I live without you?
Come up to me, love,
Out of the river, or I will
Come down to you.

Wright echoes the anonymous ballad "The Unquiet Grave" in this poem, melding his grief with his love. Just as the speaker in "The Unquiet Grave" refuses to accept the death of his beloved, proclaiming, "I'll do as much for my true-love,/ As any young man may;/ I'll sit and mourn all at the grave/ For a twelvemonth and a day," Wright's speaker also maintains his steadfast, futile vigil at Jenny's cenotaph. In both these poems, death holds the beloved hostage in the underworld. But there is no antiphonal response in Wright's "To The Muse" as there is in "The Unquiet Grave." Unlike the admonishing voice of the beloved in "The Unquiet Grave," Jenny remains silent and "alone," leaving the poem's speaker utterly disconsolate, with only himself to rely on for an answer, which he poses in the form of a question: "How can I live without you?" Wright has rubbed directly against the limit of his human understanding here, which is also the boundary of the lyric. He is intent on getting down the recrudescent expression of his most immediate feelings in the wake of Jenny's drowning. No Wordsworthian strategy of recalling emotion later in tranquility here; rather raw, unbridled love and grief infusing Wright with the inherent poetic expression of an Orphic speaker intent on leading his beloved "back to this world." But unlike Orpheus, he utters an ultimatum that betrays the madness of his grief: "Come up to me, love,/ Out of the river, or I will/ Come down to you." Precedents for such romantic suicide occur in every age as testimonies to the extreme measure lovers are willing to undertake, viewing death as an afterlife free from the "scurvy," disaster and impossibility of "this world."

This poem, however, is less about suicidality than survival through poetry. Wright's muse does "come up" to the speaker in the poem, just as he goes down to her, knowing "the place" where she lies. She inspires an Orphic music in him that decries this world, where contingency conspires with circumstance to wreak havoc on love. The enjambments throughout the poem betray the fractious, run-on nature of the speaker's voice. Breakage and violence instill his keening with heart-breaking tones, conveying both the velocity and urgency of his futile address to Jenny. This poem depends almost solely on voice for its evocation, so the speaker's convulsive voice dictates the short, tantrum-like lines that pivot on pregnant adverbs, verbs and nouns. Wright's high wire act lies in his carefully wrought, yet raw free verse that follows the uneven breaths of his love and grief. In both form and content, the poem testifies at every turn to the heroic power of witnessing over death; the chthonic details in stanza six, "the unbelievable silk of spring" and "the black sand," are the subterranean stuff of the underworld that the speaker knows and names. Like Orpheus, the speaker has been to the underworld and spoken to Hades. He "admits everything." And like Orpheus, he attempts to lead his dead beloved out of the Powhatan pit "back to this world." Wright's landscape, therefore, is both real and mythological here. The Powhatan pit is the suckhole where Jenny died, as well as the underworld out of which she emerges to "poise alone/ With me on the shore."

But what to do with Jenny once she has been led back? Wright creates a torturous, visceral conceit for this resurrected suicide (we surmise she is a suicide from the speaker's forgiving line, "I don't blame you," in the last stanza) rather than "disappearing" her a la Eurydice. The speaker escorts his love to the night office of the "three lady doctors in Wheeling" who "are always there." What happens to her there is hideous and mysterious. She is tortured at the hands of the lady doctors, who resemble the three fates.

> They hang their contraption.
> And you bear it.
> It's a while. Still, it lets you
> Walk about on tiptoe if you don't
> Jiggle the needle.
> It might stab your heart, you see.
> The blade hangs in your lung and the tube
> Keeps it draining.
> That way they only have to stab you
> Once.

But no soothsaying takes place in the lady doctors' office. Jenny is less of an oracle than a forbidden returnee from the underworld. Inanna removes her clothes and enters a bardo state in order to meet with her sister Erishkegal in hell. Osiris lives inside a pillar as the result of Isis's brother, Seth, entombing him there. Persephone resides for six months in hell with Hades after eating his pomegranate seeds. Eurydice disappears in the cave entrance at Erebus. In his own private myth in "To The Muse," Wright subjects the lost beloved, Jenny, to the ghastly machinations of the three lady doctors in Wheeling. The procedure that Wright describes is not an autopsy but an array of anomalous surgeries and "treatments" that no doctor would even recognize. The "contraption" in which Jenny must "tiptoe" around in in order to prevent the needle from stabbing her heart is a weird, nonsensical device that Wright purposefully avoids identifying lest he ruin the hierophantic mystery of his own myth. The three priestesses, who masquerade as dominatrix-like doctors in Wheeling, West Virginia, safeguard life's impossibility for the grievous speaker by imprisoning her in an office straight out of a David Lynch film. Jenny exists in two realms at once, as a resurrected but suspended body locked in a torture "contraption" at the threshold, and a dead girl friend in the Powhatan suckhole. Jenny's beloved perceives her in both places, creating the conceit of her resurrection as a palpable vision of his grief, an original metaphor of an archetypal journey to the underworld. She is a delicately balanced, booby-trapped cipher who speaks under great duress, with a "blade" pressed against her heart. (What a poignantly accurate description of Wright's own psyche as conveyed again and again in his deeply emotional poems that chronicle the "intensest rendezvous.") Death is the impossibility in the poem-the inconceivable reality of the loss of the beloved-that also renders life impossible for the speaker. Without her, he feels utterly abandoned in "this world" he has no control over, whose inexorable forces abrogate his deepest needs with chilling disregard. And yet ironically, it is only in this very world, "this scurvy and disastrous place" that the Orphic singer can sing, expressing the pathos that emanates directly from his experience of life's impossibility and unknowing. Indeed, the image of Jenny suspended in the lady doctors' anomalous contraption not only works as a mythological symbol of the lost beloved's unsuccessful return to this world, but as a vicarious evocative image as well that captures both the visceral/psychic reality of grief and abandonment. Jenny is the lost one, but the devastated surviving speaker is the one, not Jenny, who feels drained, suspended, and eviscerated.

SAD FRIEND

In a letter dated 21 March 1972, Elizabeth Bishop wrote one of her most anguished letters to her old friend Robert Lowell. For the first time in the course of their long friendship, Bishop felt that Lowell had committed a serious poetic transgression by blurring the lines between the private facts of his wife's letters and the fiction of his new poems in *The Dolphin*. While continuing to admire his poetry and respect him as a dear friend, she hardened with strong resolve against the license he took with Elizabeth Hardwick's letters for the uses of his poetry:

> I've been trying to write you this letter for weeks…It's hell to write this, so please first do believe I think *Dolphin* is magnificent poetry, It is also honest poetry-almost. You probably know already what my reactions are. I have one tremendous and awful BUT…Here is a quotation from dear little Hardy that I copied out years ago-long before *Dolphin*, or even the *Notebooks*, were thought of. It's from a letter written in 1911, referring to "an abuse which was said to have occurred-that of publishing details of a lately deceased man's life under the guise of a novel, with assurances of truth scattered in the newspapers." (Not exactly the same situation as *Dolphin* but fairly close.)
>
> "What should certainly be protested against, in cases where there is no authorization, is the mixing of fact and fiction in unknown proportions. Infinite mischief would lie in that. If any statements in the dress of fiction are covertly hinted to be fact, all must be fact, and nothing else but fact for obvious reasons. The power of getting lies believed about people through that channel after they are dead, by stirring in a few truths, is a horror to contemplate."
>
> I'm sure my point is only too plain. Lizzie is not dead, etc.- but there is a "mixture of fact & fiction," and you have changed her letters. That is "infinite mischief," I think.

Bishop's affectionate reference to a letter by "dear little Hardy" in her criticism of *The Dolphin* betrays her old world propriety. But her reaction to *The Dolphin* is significant for more than her moral objection to Lowell's indiscriminate use of Hardwick's letters. It reflects equally her commitment to a non-confessional poetic strategy. The idea of bastardizing personal letters in one's poetry was unacceptable to Bishop for reasons that informed her own aesthetic as, in the words of Helen McNeil, a "lifelong attention to the phenomenology of perception." To better understand this aesthetic and how it grew out of Bishop's moral development, it is enlightening to review her fierce correspondence with Lowell.

In Robert Giroux's book *One Art*, a collection of Bishop's selected and edited letters, one is struck repeatedly by Bishop's fierce sanity. Although she at times envies Lowell for his family's prestige, she maintains a stalwart sense of her unassuming, perspicacious self. In a letter dated December 14, 1957, fifteen years prior to her critique of *The Dolphin*, she wrote this candid admission to Lowell:

> ...I must confess (and I imagine most of our contemporaries would confess the same thing) that I am green with envy of your kind of assurance. I feel that I could write in as much detail about my uncle Artie, say-but what would be the significance? Nothing at all...Whereas all you have to do is put down the names! And the fact that it seems significant, illustrative, American, etc., give you, I think, the confidence you display about tackling any idea of theme, seriously, in both writing and conversation. IN some ways you are the luckiest poet I know!- in some ways not so lucky, either, of course. But it is hell to realize one has wasted half one's talent through timidity that probably could have been overcome if anyone in one's family had had a few grains of sense or education. Well, maybe it's not too late!

This said, Bishop then adds a disclaimer that preserves her sense of objectivity with a note of generosity:

> I'm not really complaining and of course am not really "jealous" in any deep sense at all. I've felt almost as wonderful a sense of relief since I first saw some of these poems in Boston as if I'd written them myself, and I've thought of them at off times and places with the greatest pleasure every single day since, I swear.

This rare confession conveys the disparity Bishop felt throughout her friendship with Lowell between her own middle-class, orphan background and Lowell's Brahmin heritage. There are numerous other humble references to herself scattered throughout her letters to Lowell and others, some in fact shocking for their honesty. "I'm sorry I can't seem to say all the right things I'd like to. I really should learn to be more articulate, I know" (December 14, 1957 letter quoted above); "When you write my epitaph, you must say I was the loneliest person who ever lived" (August 15, 1957, to Lowell); "I'm getting so I can't judge the poets we know so well any more at all…Your life sounds very nice and well peopled. Mine has been rather lonely and bookish but I don't really care much" (October 30, 1958, to Lowell). Bishop's stability and clearheaded advice were invaluable to Lowell, prompting him even to contemplate proposing to her. In a letter dated August 15, 1957, Lowell expressed his unbridled gratitude to her: "Your advice about [my] going to a doctor and keeping up one's patience, sobriety, toughness, and gaiety is dreadfully true, and I am sure that all is beginning to be well. In this same letter, Lowell confessed an old desire to propose to Bishop in 1948:

> The possible alternatives that life allows us are very few, often there must be none. I've never thought there was any choice for me about writing poetry…But asking you is the might-have-been for me, the one towering change, the other life that might have been had. It was that way for these nine years or so that intervened. It was deeply buried, and this spring and summer (really before you arrival) it boiled to the surface.

Bishop never responded to this belated news, choosing instead to preserve the intimate, Platonic nature of their friendship.

The tension between Bishop's diminutive sense of herself and Lowell's aristocratic swagger didn't become problematic until 1972, when Lowell published *The Dolphin*. With so little ego in her poetry, Bishop relied on patient, brilliant observation to achieve frissons of self-awareness. Lowell praised her work by referring to "the bomb in it in a delicate way." However, the idea of confession as a muse for Bishop was as foreign to her as the nothing of assuming an aristocratic identity. She is perhaps the most Keatsian American poet of the twentieth century in her capacity "to live in uncertainty with no irritable reaching." Her negative capability, while a prodigious poetic strength, was also a reflection discovering itself in such unlikely objects as those highlighted in "In the Waiting Room," namely the "awful hanging breasts" of African women in the National Geographic and her foolish Aunt Consuelo.

The thought of complaining or confessing ran counter to both Bishop's central ethic of survival, which was to adopt a persevering but compassionate stoicism, and her poetic strategy, which was to discover bright truths behind the subterfuge of ordinary life and suffering. In her persona poem, "Crusoe in England," Bishop constructs perhaps her most incisive idea of the solitary self as an exile subsumed by the strangeness of the world. The poem is a plangent reminiscence in which Crusoe recalls the salient features of his island, finding reminders of home in both the landscape and the creatures of his "cloud dump."

> The turtles lumbered by, high domed,
> Hissing like teakettles
> ………………..
> The folds of lava, running out to sea,
> Would hiss…

He harvests the red berries of the island in order to concoct a crude cocktail.

> Sub-acid, and not bad, no ill effects;
> And so I made home-brew. I'd drink
> The awful, fizzy, stinging stuff
> That went straight to my head.

But for all his ingenuity, he remains unabashedly self-pitying in the absence of his usual comforts, confessing:

> With my legs dangling down familiarly
> Over a crater's edge, I told myself
> "Pity should begin at home." So the more
> Pity I felt, the more I felt at home.

He is overwhelmed by the sudden terrible awareness of his smallness on an unnamed, volcanic island that he dreams is like

> …other islands
> Stretching away from mine, infinities

Of islands, islands spawning islands,
Like frogs' eggs turning into polliwogs
Of islands…

Crusoe suffers from a deep insecurity that isn't assuaged until he is saved from his brown studies by Friday.

Just when I thought I couldn't stand it
Another minute longer, Friday came.
(Accounts of that have everything all wrong.)
Friday was nice.
Friday was nice, and we were friends.

By repeating "nice" in lieu of such terms as wonderful or dear or beloved, Crusoe is in fact making an awkward attempt at professing his deep affection for Friday. (Interestingly, Bishop's repetition of "nice" echoes D.H. Lawrence's parodic use of this word in his poem "The English Are So Nice.") Without Friday, Crusoe simply remains a pathetic castaway. Although indigenous, strange, and uncivilized, Friday provides an essential human point of connection for Crusoe's lost self. He laments that Friday is not a woman since he wished "to propagate his own kind" with him, as he thinks Friday also wished to do with him. The language is remarkable elementary in the stanza about Friday, as if Crusoe is at a regrettable loss to express his intimate feelings toward his new friend. Yet, his diminished sense of self is saved from the vortex of the island's ironic vastness, made larger for its indifference strangeness. Back in England, his other island, Crusoe languishes with a seemingly greater ennui than the one he suffered on his "cloud dump."

I'm bored, too, drinking my real tea,
surrounded by uninteresting lumber.
....
The living soul has dribbled away.

The poem ends with the news of Friday's death from measles "seventeen years ago come March." Ironically, unlike Crusoe who survives the elements and germs of his former strange new world with a knife and fortitude, Friday succumbs quickly to a common occidental disease. But a memorable epiphany resounds beyond the poem's elegiac conclusion. Crusoe was at least momentarily transformed from a whining, lone survivor to a joyous friend. Bishop created an apotheosis in Crusoe of the found self within the other. Unlike the speakers in Lowell's "Skunk Hour" or "Waking in the Blue," where the self remains marooned, solitary, and deranged, Crusoe finds a way out of his self-pity though his genuine if awkward appreciation of Friday's ordinary acts.

He'd pet the baby goats sometimes,
And race with them, or carry one around.

Lowell's exploitation of his wife's letters for poetic purposes bothered Bishop because he "changed" the text. Since revelation for Bishop relied on the sovereign otherness of her subject matter, she divined knowledge in an inexorable world "derived from the rocky breasts/ forever, flowing and flown, and since/ our knowledge is historical, flowing, and flown" ("At the Fishhouses"). Elizabeth Hardwick's letters were not dissimilar from the "rocky breasts," for they were authored by another, to be perceived and apprehended but not changed. By changing Hardwick's letters in *The Dolphin*, Lowell was in Bishop's eyes committing the "indefinite mischief" of superimposing his powerful will onto his subject matter rather than allowing it to speak for itself. In addition to violating his wife's privacy, Lowell was also misrepresenting himself, avoiding the kind of essential self-discovery that occurs through close identification with something altogether other and strange. By interpreting the world on its own rhetorical terms, Lowell denied himself the opportunity of arriving at a full realization of himself as a paradoxical being, both individual and other, as the young speaker so succinctly does in "In the Waiting Room" when she proclaims "you are an I, / you are an Elizabeth,/ you are one of them. /Why should you be one, too?"

This impasse, unfortunately, was never resolved between them, prompting Bishop to address it directly in her memorial poem for Lowell titled "North Haven." Setting up her farewell stanza with the recent pastoral news for Lowell's Innisfree, she concludes by addressing him directly with plangent honesty:

> You left North Haven, anchored in its rock
> afloat in mystic blue...And now- you've left
> for good. You can't derange, or re-arrange,
> your poems again. (But the Sparrows can their song.)
> The words won't change again. Sad friend, you cannot change.

Bishop's affection for Lowell radiates from these lines with such powerful sympathy that any residual distress she may have felt over his altering ways is transformed into tender elegy. Her past judgment is overridden by her repetitive acknowledgement of death's final word. She suspends her moral condemnation of Lowell's indiscriminate use of sources in order to find a way to accept his poetic tricksterism. By parenthetically echoing Keats's trans-historical nightingale, with perhaps a veiled reference to herself as “the Sparrows,” Bishop discerns the rightful order between “words” and birdsong: the former are intransigent, while the latter is timeless and free. It is precisely this wisdom that imbues her elegy with transcendent affection and truth. She converts what would have appeared as a sharp criticism in life–“You can’t derange, or re-arrange,/ your poems again”–into memorable pathos.

SILENCE AMIDST THE CROWD, A READING OF PHILIP LEVINE'S "THE SIMPLE TRUTH" AND "CALL IT MUSIC"

Two remarkably patient, self-effacing poems that invoke the unsayable in the midst of America's increasingly bumptious culture are "The Simple Truth" and "Call It Music" by Philip Levine. Although appearing ten years apart, "The Simple Truth" in 1994 and "Call It Music" in 2004, these two lyrical narratives defer in their conclusions to the ineffable "voice" behind speech, moving from a remorseful ars poetica in "The Simple Truth" to a mystical reverie in "Call It Music." In both poems, the catalyst that inspires Levine to humble himself before ineffable truths lies in his placing others, a potato vender in "The Simple Truth" and Charlie Parker in "Call It Music," before him with Whitman-like awe and empathy. It is Levine's "negative capability" in identifying with these sacred ordinary others that spawns his awareness of the power of the unsayable.

The Simple Truth

I bought a dollar and a half's worth of small red potatoes,
took them home, boiled them in their jackets
and ate them for dinner with a little butter and salt.
Then I walked through the dried fields
on the edge of town. In the middle of June the light
hung on in the dark furrows at my feet,
and in the mountain oaks overhead the birds
were gathering for the night, the jays and mockers
squawking back and forth, the finches still darting
into the dusty light. The woman who sold me the potatoes
was from Poland; she was someone
out of my childhood in a pink spangled sweater and sunglasses
praising the perfection of all her fruits and vegetables
at the road-side stand and urging me to taste

even the pale, raw sweet corn trucked all the way,
she swore, from New Jersey. "Eat, eat," she said,
"Even if you don't I'll say you did."
                                                            Some things
you know all your life. They are so simple and true
they must be said without elegance, meter and rhyme,
they must be laid on the table beside the salt-shaker,
the glass of water, the absence of light gathering
in the shadows of picture frames, they must be
naked and alone, they must stand for themselves.
My friend Henri and I arrived at this together in 1965
before I went away, before he began to kill himself,
and the two of us betray our love. Can you taste
what I'm saying? It is onions and potatoes, a pinch
of simple salt, the wealth of melting butter, it is obvious,
it stays in the back of your throat like a truth
you never uttered because the time was always wrong,
it stays there for the rest of your life, unspoken,
made of that dirt we call earth, the metal we call salt,
in a form we have no words for, and you live in it.

Call It Music

Some days I catch a rhythm, almost a song
in my own breath. I'm alone here
in Brooklyn, it's late morning, the sky
above the St. George Hotel is clear, clear
for New York, that is. The radio is playing
Bird Flight. Parker in his California
tragic voice fifty years ago, his faltering

“Lover Man” just before he crashed into chaos.
I would guess that outside the recording studio
in Burbank the sun was high above the jacarandas,
it was late March, the worst of yesterday’s rain
had come and gone, the sky was washed. Bird
could have seen for miles if he’d looked, but what
he saw was so foreign he clenched his eyes,
shook his head, and barked like a dog-just once-
and then Howard McGhee took his arm and assured him
he’d be OK. I know this because Howard told me
years later, told me he thought Bird could
lie down in the hotel room they shared, sleep
for an hour or more, and waken as himself.
The perfect sunlight angles into my little room
above Willow Street. I listen to my breath
come and go and try to catch its curious taste,
part milk, part iron, part blood, as it passes
from me into the world. This is not me,
this is automatic, this entering and exiting,
my body’s essential occupation without which
I am a thing. The whole process has a name,
a word I don’t know, an elegant word not
in English and Yiddish or Spanish, a word
that means nothing to me. Howard truly believed
what he said that day when he steered
Parker into a cab and drove the silent miles
beside him while the bright world
unfurled around them: filling stations, stands
of fruits and vegetables, a kiosk selling trinkets
from Mexico and the Philippines. It was all
so actual and Western, it was a new creation

coming into being, like the music of Charlie Parker
someone later called "glad," though that day
I would have said silent, "the silent music
of Charlie Parker." Howard said nothing.
He paid the driver and helped Bird up two flights
to their room, got his boots off, and went out
to let him sleep as the afternoon entered
the history of darkness. I'm not judging
Howard, he did better than I could have
now or then. Then I was nineteen, working
on the loading docks at Railway Express,
coming day by day into the damaged body
of a man while I sang into the filthy air
the Yiddish drinking songs my Zadie taught me
before his breath failed. Now Howard is gone,
eleven years gone, the sweet voice silenced.
"The subtle bridge between Eldridge and Navarro,"
they later wrote, all that rising passion
a footnote to others, I remember in '85
walking the halls of Cass Tech, the high school
where he taught after his performing days,
when suddenly he took my left hand in his
two hands to tell me it all worked out
for the best. Maybe he'd gotten religion,
maybe he knew how little time was left,
maybe that day he was just worn down
by my questions about Parker. To him Bird
was truly Charlie Parker, a man, a silent note
going out forever on the breath of genius
which now I hear soaring above my own breath
as this bright morning fades into afternoon.

Music, I'll call it music. It's what we need
as the sun staggers behind the low gray clouds
blowing relentlessly in from the nameless ocean,
the calm and endless one I've still to cross.

These two poems develop similar paradoxical themes on the nature of Levine's inscrutable muse. While issuing a prophet-like caveat at the close of "The Simple Truth" about the impossibility of ever speaking truths he's known "all his life," despite their life-sustaining presence in the "back of the throat," in "a form we have no words for," Levine defines this unspeakable but palpable truth in "Call It Music" as "a silent note/ going out forever on the breath of genius." Although generally not given to philosophical flights in his recurring lyrical narratives and jeremiads about factory work, family history, anti-Semitism, the legacy of poetry and rites of passage, Levine conjures a metaphysical conceit for music that is similar to his conceit for truth, an abiding, mystical silence. A close reading of these poems reveals an overheard voice that engages Levine in a poetic conversation with himself about just what he can and cannot say. But his subject, which is also not a subject, namely, those truths that are inexpressible, remains the inscrutable subtext of both poems and consequently Levine's essential agon in the making of these poems.

Levine divides "The Simple Truth" into two sections with the strategy of broaching his impossible subject by first engaging his reader with personal narrative. In the first seventeen lines of the poem, he recounts a recent purchase of "a dollar and a half's worth of small red potatoes" from a Polish woman-"someone out of [his] childhood"-and then walking through "the dried fields on the edge of town" in June. While this vignette is rich with pastoral detail, recalling a scene out of Dos Passos' *USA* or a passage from

Whitman's "Democratic Vistas," it doesn't present much more than a vivid account of Levine's encounter with a Polish vender at a roadside vegetable stand who urges him to "eat, eat" her fruits and vegetables. This woman's look, accent and threat bring back memories of Levine's childhood, prompting him to turn his reflection into philosophizing. Moving from the Polish woman's command to "eat, eat" to the general observation that there are "some things you know all your life," Levine unravels an ars poetica that redounds on the very chthonic ground he describes so evocatively in the first half of the poem. The literal potatoes he bought for "a dollar and a half" from the Polish woman become metaphors for the unsayable, which are those "things" one knows all his life. This a priori epistemology becomes the real subject of the poem, addressing the poet's primary responsibility to innate knowledge, namely, to forgo "elegance, meter and rhyme" when speaking of those things "so simple and true." What remains mysterious, however, is why this awareness about the simple truth leads to suicide and betrayal. Levine confesses his and Henri's betrayal of their love, along with Henri's suicidal downward spiral, as a seemingly direct consequence of his awareness of the truth's need for simple and inelegant form. "My friend Henri and I arrived at this together in 1965/ before I went away, before he began to kill himself,/ and the two of us to betray our love." Levine leads his reader to assume from these tragic consequences of arriving at the simple truth, that it, whatever "it" is, is both revelatory and destructive.

Levine's shift from literal story-telling to figurative witnessing turns on his phrase "some things" in line 18. By implication, these "things" are antipodes of formal poetic expression, free of meter and elegance. Things (lines, phrases, silence) that "stand for themselves...naked and alone...on the table beside the salt shaker." But Levine never says what these things are specifically, leaving his reader to surmise for herself. He does, however, provide gustatory clues that hearken back to the potatoes he bought from the Polish hierophant at the roadside vegetable stand and went home and cooked for dinner "with a little butter and salt." These same potatoes are now "like a truth you never uttered because the time was always wrong." The same food that's celebrated for its sustenance at the start of the poem has now become "like a truth" "at the back of the throat." We now see what Levine was up to in the first part of the poem, namely setting up the physical "that" with his potato vignette in a dialectic that concludes with a metaphysical "this" that incorporates the same potato. Patience leads to prescience in this compound narrative where earth is wed to truth "in a form we have no words for" but nonetheless exists as a vital sustenance that one lives on, or not. The elusive simple truth Levine leaves his reader with resonates more as a spiritual cognizance than any possible truthful utterance. The fact that the "time is always wrong" for uttering those things one knows all his life belies any absolute efficacy of language, leaving silence as truth's most authentic realm and poetry's inscrutable, ironic source.

A decade after writing "The Simple Truth," Levine returned to silence in his poem "Call It Music" as a realm that evinces more than mere absence of sound, but a mystical music as well that resonates first from random things in "the bright world," then finds its way through the receptive ear and eye of the musician to an adequate instrument, which Levine identifies as Charlie Parker's saxophone. And even though this silent music emanating from mere ordinary things pours out ultimately from Parker's saxophone, Levine claims that it somehow also remains "silent."

Howard truly believed
what he said that day when he steered

> Parker into a cab and drove the silent miles
> beside him while the bright world
> unfurled around them: filling stations, stands
> of fruits and vegetables, a kiosk selling trinkets
> from Mexico and the Philippines. It was all
> so actual and Western, it was a new creation
> coming into being, like the music of Charlie Parker
> someone later called "glad," though that day
> I would have said silent, "the silent music
> of Charlie Parker." Howard said nothing.

Whether intentional or not, Levine echoes here the same ancient conceit that David employs in lines 2 through 4 of Psalm 19. "Day to day pours forth speech,/ and night to night declares knowledge. There is no speech, nor are there words;/ their voice is not heard;/ yet their voice goes out through all the earth,/ and their words to the end of the world." Substitute Parker's saxophone in this Psalm for "day" and "night," and one becomes the other. This metaphorical synergy that Levine's friend, Larry Levis, called "glad music" does indeed play out as "day's speech" and "night's knowledge" in "Call It Music," betraying his inherent awareness-not unlike David's-of the ultimate "silence" of his own words within time's cosmic sweep. But it is this particular submission and admission that imbrue Levine's lines in the here and now with valiant witness to the "bright world," the glittering minutiae and "glad music" that is memorable, at least for as long as his "voice" and lines remain in the memories of his readers.

Levine repeats the same gustatory metaphor in "Call It Music" that he used in "The Simple Truth" to once again capture the taste of truth, equating it to the air that sustains him. "I listen to my breath/ come and go and try to catch its curious taste,/ part milk, part iron, part blood." Can one then infer syllogistically that truth is breath for Levine? Or does he merely wish to use the same metaphor to describe both truth and breath while ascribing different meanings to these two subjects? He does add milk and blood to the list, so there are a few additional flavors in his organic taste. But Levine never makes any definitive claim about truth being breath, or vice versa, choosing instead to distill his tropes in "Call It Music" (the last poem in most recent book titled Breath) down to four things: "automatic" breath, a "curious taste" silent music, and the "breath of genius." Levine writes about these four endogenous and metaphysical things as if he has known them all his life, but is just now finding the right words for his mystical knowledge. He talks to himself throughout much of the poem, overhearing himself say that his breathing is not he, that Charlie Parker's music is "silent," that his late friend Howard McGhee, a jazz musician, teacher and disciple of Charlie Parker, did the best he could in attending to Parker, despite Parker's institutionalization and early demise, and that the word for the "whole process" of breathing "means nothing" to him. In a show of exemplary deference, Levine humbles himself before Parker's music at the end of the poem, perceiving from his humility's ironic alembic just what ineffable quality Parker's music possesses that inspires him in turn to call it "silent," namely, its genius "above [his] own breath." Levine qualifies this music as necessary, not just for him, but for his reader as well. "It's what we need/ as the sun staggers behind the low gray clouds/ blowing relentlessly in from the nameless ocean." However, rather than issue another directive about the inexpressible, as he does in "The Simple Truth," Levine returns to his first person musing, concluding with a deferential acknowledgment of "that nameless ocean/ that calm and endless one I've still to cross."

The poem has been personal up to this point, elegizing the lives and music of Howard McGhee and Charlie Parker. Levine's leap from I to we at the end betrays his subtle but effective shift away from the personal to the universal, saving the poem from mere private reminiscence about his two late friends and his own imminent demise. Unlike his speaker in "The Simple Truth" who leaves his reader with a palpable metaphor for the "unsayable," Levine avoids the topic of telling "the simple truth" altogether in his conclusion of "Call It Music" in favor of evincing the power of breath alone as that transcendent ether that both vivifies the body and sounds "the silent notes" of genius.

The metaphor in the poem's diminuendo is revelatory for Levine. Charlie Parker the man, who is also "a silent note going out forever on the breath of genius" leads Levine like an angel to the inner sanctum of silent music where he hears Parker's breath "soaring above [his] own" at day's end. This music's inherent grace, in turn, bestows a mortal vision to Levine of an empyreal ocean, "the calm and endless one [he has] still to cross." Like Dickinson's psychopomp, a fly "with blue uncertain stumbling buzz" in her poem "I heard a fly buzz," Parker's silent music leads Levine to that point where he "cannot see to see." And yet he does see a final time and place, at least in his mind; it is an afternoon at the beach on a cloudy afternoon, but like the truth he cannot utter in "The Simple Truth," the ocean over which the clouds blow in concealing the sun, remains nameless.

Levine's patience with his impossible subject lies in his wisdom to submit to truths he knows but cannot express, "without any irritable reaching after fact or reason." His willful surrender to "the silent note" instills him with a self-abnegating muse. In a letter Levine wrote to me about this poem in response to a first draft of this essay, he provided this invaluable footnote on the inspiration of Parker's music within the tragic context of his abbreviated life.

The silent music of Charlie Parker. Have you ever heard the recording--that famous infamous one--of "Lover Man"? It's one Bird wished was never released. It was Larry Levis who used the term "the glad music" of Bird. I say silent because that solo says so much about silence, and then it was followed by months of literal silence because Parker was confined to a mental institution in Camarillo, California for close to six months. When near the end of the poem I hear Bird's voice soaring above my own, I'm hearing his music; in the beginning of the poem I refer to "Bird Flight"--that's a week-day radio broadcast hosted by Phil Schaap on WKCR; it lasts over an hour and is dedicated to the music of Charlie Parker...The poem is about what cannot be said. I have for some years been writing about just this theme.

Levine is not alone among other poets of his generation in his homage to the unsayable. Adrienne Rich and W.S. Merwin corroborate his paradoxical embrace of the unsayable in recent testimonies of their own. Adrienne Rich concludes her 2006 essay "Poetry and Commitment" with this reaffirmation of the timeless role of "the unspeakable" in poetry. "Finally: there is always that in poetry which will not be grasped, which cannot be described, which survives our ardent attention, our critical theories, our classrooms, our late night arguments. There is always (I am quoting the poet/translator Americo Ferrari) 'an unspeakable where, perhaps, the nucleus of the living relation between the poem and the world resides.'" W.S. Merwin echoes Rich's sentiments in a prepared statement on this subject that appeared in the *American Poetry Review's* 25th Anniversary issue last summer (June/July 2008). Responding to the question, How does poetry help people to live their lives?, Merwin answered, "The source that rises unbroken from the unsayable speaks to us of the impulse and mystery that we share with every living creature. The urge is meaningless, like the unknown itself, and in the end remains, by nature, unsayable." While these statements reaffirm what is most sacred about the wellspring of poetry in eloquent prose, Levine's testimonies to what Qoholeth described in *Ecclesiastes* as the "eternity that God has put into the minds of men, but so he cannot figure out what has happened from beginning to end," provides a timely poetic update on the inviolate silence that resounds between the lines of memorable poetry.

BIOGRAPHICAL NOTES

Donald Hall

Donald Hall was born in New Haven, Connecticut, in 1928. He began writing as an adolescent and attended the Bread Loaf Writers' Conference at the age of sixteen—the same year he had his first work published. He earned a B.A. from Harvard in 1951 and a B. Litt. from Oxford in 1953. Donald Hall has published numerous books of poetry, most recently *White Apples and the Taste of Stone: Selected Poems 1946-2006* (Houghton Mifflin, 2006); *The Painted Bed* (2002) and *Without: Poems* (1998), which was published on the third anniversary of his wife and fellow poet Jane Kenyon's death from leukemia. Other notable collections include *The One Day* (1988), which won the National Book Critics Circle Award, the Los Angeles Times Book Prize, and a Pulitzer Prize nomination; *The Happy Man* (1986), which won the Lenore Marshall Poetry Prize; and *Exiles and Marriages* (1955), which was the Academy's Lamont Poetry Selection for 1956.

Besides poetry, Donald Hall has written books on baseball, the sculptor Henry Moore, and the poet Marianne Moore. He is also the author of children's books, including *Ox-Cart Man* (1979), which won the Caldecott Medal; short stories, including *Willow Temple: New and Selected Stories* (Houghton Mifflin, 2003); and plays. He has also published several autobiographical works, such as *The Best Day The Worst Day: Life with Jane Kenyon* (2005) and *Life Work* (1993), which won the New England Book award for nonfiction and *Unpacking the Boxes, a Memoir of a Life in Poetry*, published in 2009.

Hall has edited more than two dozen textbooks and anthologies, including *The Oxford Book of Children's Verse in America* (1990), *The Oxford Book of American Literary Anecdotes* (1981), *New Poets of England and America* (with Robert Pack and Louis Simpson,

1957), and *Contemporary American Poetry* (1962; revised 1972). He served as poetry editor of *The Paris Review* from 1953 to 1962, and as a member of editorial board for poetry at Wesleyan University Press from 1958 to 1964.

His honors include two Guggenheim fellowships, the Poetry Society of America's Robert Frost Silver medal, a Lifetime Achievement award from the New Hampshire Writers and Publisher Project, and the Ruth Lilly Prize for poetry. Hall also served as Poet Laureate of New Hampshire from 1984 to 1989. In December 1993 he and Jane Kenyon were the subject of an Emmy Award-winning Bill Moyers documentary, "A Life Together." In the June 2006, Hall was appointed the Library of Congress's fourteenth Poet Laureate Consultant in Poetry.

Donald Hall lives in his eighties on an old family farm in Danbury, New Hampshire. His last book of poems, *The Back Chamber*, will appear in September of 2011. There will be further publications in prose.

From The Academy of American Poets Web site Poetry.org.

Galway Kinnell

Galway Kinnell is the author of ten books of poetry, including *Body Rags, The Book of Nightmares, Mortal Acts, Mortal Words, The Past, When One Has Lived a Long Time Alone, Imperfect Thirst,* and most recently *Strong is Your Hold.* He also published a novel, *Black Light,* a selection of interviews, *Walking Down the Stairs,* and a book for children, as well as translations of works by Yves Bonnefoy, Yvan Goll, Francois Villon and Rainer Maria Rilke, and edited *The Essential Whitman.*

Born in 1927 in Providence, Rhode Island, he was raised in Pawtucket, graduated summa cum laude from Princeton University, served in the Navy, and took a Masters degree from University of Rochester. From 1951-55, he was the director of the adult education program at the University of Chicago's Downtown Center. As a Fulbright Lecturer he taught at both the University of Grenoble in France in 1956-57 and at the University of Tehran in Iran in 1959-60. He was a field worker for the Congress of Racial Equality in Hammond, Louisiana and a field worker for the Student Non-Violent Coordinating Committee in Montgomery, Alabama in 1963 and 1964. A former MacArthur Fellow and State Poet of Vermont, he has served as a Chancellor of The Academy of American Poets. In 1982, his *Selected Poems* won both the Pulitzer Prize and the National Book Award; A *New Selected Poems* was published in 2000. He was awarded the Shelley Prize and the Frost Medal by the Poetry Society of America, and the 2010 Wallace Stevens Award from the Academy of American Poetry. He taught for many years at New York University, where he was Erich Maria Remarque Professor of Creative Writing. He lives in northern Vermont.

Robert Bly

Robert Bly was born in western Minnesota in 1926 to parents of Norwegian stock. He enlisted in the Navy in 1944 and spent two years there. After one year at St. Olaf College in Minnesota, he transferred to Harvard and thereby joined the famous group of writers who were undergraduates at that time, which included Donald Hall, Adrienne Rich, Kenneth Koch, John Ashbery, Harold Brodky, George Plimpton, and John Hawkes. He graduated in 1950 and spent the next few years in New York living, as they say, hand to mouth.

Beginning in 1954, he took two years at the University of Iowa at the Writers Workshop along with W. D. Snodgrass, Donald Justice, and others. In 1956 he received a Fulbright grant to travel to Norway and translate Norwegian poetry into English. While there he found not only his relatives but the work of a number of major poets whose force was not present in the United States, among them Pablo Neruda, Cesar Vallejo, Gunnar Ekelof, Georg Trakl and Harry Martinson. He determined then to start a literary magazine for poetry translation in the United States and so begin *The Fifties* and *The Sixties* and *The Seventies*, which introduced many of these poets to the writers of his generation, and published as well essays on American poets and insults to those deserving. During this time he lived on a farm in Minnesota with his wife and children.

In 1966 he co-founded American Writers Against the Vietnam War and led much of the opposition among writers to that war. When he won the National Book Award for *The Light Around the Body*, he contributed the prize money to the Resistance.

During the 70s he published eleven books of poetry, essays, and translations, celebrating the power of myth, Indian ecstatic poetry, meditation, and storytelling.

During the 80s he published *Loving a Woman in Two Worlds, The Wingéd Life: Selected Poems and Prose of Thoreau,The Man in the Black Coat Turns*, and *A Little Book on the Human Shadow*. His work *Iron John: A Book About Men* is an international bestseller which has been translated into many languages.

In the early 90s, with James Hillman and Michael Meade, he edited *The Rag and Bone Shop of the Heart*, an anthology of poems from the men's work. Since then he has edited *The Darkness Around Us Is Deep: Selected Poems of William Stafford*, and *The Soul Is Here for Its Own Joy*, a collection of sacred poetry from many cultures. Recent books of poetry include *What Have I Ever Lost by Dying? Collected Prose Poems and Meditations on the Insatiable Soul*, both published by Harper Collins. His second large prose book, *The Sibling Society*, published by Addison-Wesley in hardcover and Vintage in paperback, is the subject of nation-wide discussion. His collection, *Morning Poems* (Harper Collins), named for William Stafford's practice of writing a poem each morning, revisits the western Minnesota farm country of Bly's boyhood.

In the mid to late 90s, he published *The Maiden King: The Reunion of Masculine and Feminine* (Henry Holt) in collaboration with Marion Woodman. A new selected poems, *Eating the Honey of Words*, appeared in 1999 from Harper Flamingo. Recent translations include his versions of Ghalib, *The Lightning Should Have Fallen on Ghalib* (with Sunil Dutta) from Ecco Press and *Angels Knocking on the Tavern Door* (HarperCollins) a collection of poems by Hafez (with Leonard Lewisohn). Bly has also edited the prestigious *Best American Poetry 1999* (Scribners).

In 2000 he won the McKnight Foundation's Distinguished Artist Award. A book of ghazals, *The Night Abraham Called to the Stars*, was published by Harper Collins in 2001, and his selected translations, *The Winged Energy of Delight*, appeared from

HarperCollins in 2004. In 2005 HarperCollins published his second book of ghazals, *My Sentence Was a Thousand Years of Joy*.

In 2008, the Guthrie Theatre staged his translation of Ibsen's Peer Gynt. Recently, White Pine Press has published a new selection of his prose poems, *Reaching Out to the World*. Forthcoming in 2011 from W. W. Norton is a new collection of poems, *Talking into the Ear of a Donkey*.

He lives with his wife Ruth in Minneapolis.

Ruth Stone

Ruth Stone has lived and written since 1958, when she wasn't teaching to support her family, at her Goshen, Vt. home. There, in what most would consider poverty conditions—the house has no potable water in the winter —she has thrived as a poet, widow, single mother, grandmother and great grandmother until only a few years ago when her deteriorating eye sight forced her to move to an apartment in Middlebury, and then to her daughter Marcia's house in Ripton.

With her muse in one ear and the world in the other, Stone has relied throughout her career on her "vast female mind" for both poetry and survival, fiercely maintaining her matrilineal heritage along the way. "No amount of knowledge can shake my grandma out of me;/ or my Aunt Maud; or my mama, who didn't just bite an apple/ with her big white teeth. She split it in two," she writes in her poem "Pokeberries". What Stone identifies as her triple threat, namely her grandma, her aunt and her mama, has instilled in her a rare constitution and skill set, such traits as ingenuity, perseverance, a love of literature and music, and a clear sense of her destiny as a gifted, independent woman in a man's world. Because she survived her formidable hardships as a strong person foremost, particularly her husband's suicide when she was only 44, her poetry has run as a parallel river to her life's river, as she so eloquently put it in her acceptance speech for her book *In the Next Galaxy* at the 2002 National Book Award ceremony.

Ruth Stone was born on June 8, 1915, in Roanoke, Virginia. Her recent books of poetry include *What Love Comes To* (Copper Canyon Press, a finalist for the 2009 Pulitzer Prize), *In the Next Galaxy* (Copper Canyon 2002), *Ordinary Words* (Paris Press, 1999), *Simplicity* (Paris Press, 1997), *Who is the Widow's Muse* (1991),

Second Hand Coat (1987), *Cheap* (1975), *Topography* (1971), and *In an Iridescent Time* (1959). She has published poems in numerous anthologies and literary journals. Stone is the recipient of the 2002 Wallace Stevens Award. Among her other awards are two Guggenheim Fellowships, The Bess Hokin Award from Poetry magazine, the Shelley Memorial Award, the Vermont Cerf Award for lifetime achievement in the arts, the National Book Critics Circle Award, and the National Book Award. Stone was a professor of English and creative writing at Binghamton University from 1990 to 2005.

Maxine Kumin

Maxine Kumin is the author of seventeen books of poems, most recently *Where I Live: New & Selected Poems 1990-2010* (W.W. Norton), five books of essays, seven books of fiction, sixteen children's books, four of which she collaborated on with Anne Sexton, and a memoir recounting a nearly fatal carriage-driving accident that took place 1998 titled *Inside the Halo and Beyond: Anatomy of a Recovery*.

She has taught at Brandeis, MIT, Columbia, Washington University at St. Louis, Miami University in Florida, and Princeton. Her awards include the Pulitzer and Ruth Lilly Poetry Prizes, the Poet's Prize, the Aiken Taylor Award, the 2005 Harvard Arts Medal, the Robert Frost Medal in 2006, and the 2009 Paterson award for distinguished literary achievement. In 1981-2, she served as Consultant in Poetry to the Library of Congress, a post that was renamed Poet Laureate of the United States. Her husband Victor and she live on a horse farm in Warner, New Hampshire with three rescued dogs and two ancient horses.

Jack Gilbert

Born in 1925, Jack Gilbert grew up in Pittsburgh's East Liberty neighborhood and was educated at the University of Pittsburgh and San Francisco State. He spent various periods of his life outside the United States, primarily in France, Italy, and Greece, publishing infrequently. His five poetry collections include: *Views of Jeopardy* (1962), winner of the Yale Younger Poets Series; *Monolithos* (1982), a finalist for the Pulitzer Prize; *The Great Fires* (1994); *Refusing Heaven* (2005), winner of the National Book Critics Circle Award; and *The Dance Most of All* (2009). He was married to the American poet Linda Gregg and later to the Japanese poet Michiko Nogami, to whom he dedicated a limited edition of elegiac poems, *Kochan* (1984). He presently resides in Berkeley, California.

Lucille Clifton

Lucille Clifton was born in Depew, New York, on June 27, 1936. Her first book of poems, *good times*, was rated one of the best books of the year by the *New York Times* in 1969. Clifton remained employed in state and federal government positions until 1971, when she became a writer in residence at Coppin State College in Baltimore, Maryland, where she completed two collections: *good news about the earth* (1972) and *an ordinary woman* (1974).

She has gone on to write several other collections of poetry, including *voices* (BOA Editions, 2008); *mercy* (2004); *blessing the boats: new and selected poems 1988-2000* (2000), which won the National Book Award; *the terrible stories* (1995), which was nominated for the National Book Award; *the book of light* (1993); *quilting: poems 1987-1990* (1991); *next: new poems* (1987)

Her collection *good woman: poems and a memoir 1969-1980* (1987) was nominated for the Pulitzer Prize; *two-headed woman* (1980), also a Pulitzer Prize nominee, was the recipient of the University of Massachusetts Press Juniper Prize. She has also written *generations: a memoir* (1976) and more than sixteen books for children, written expressly for an African-American audience.
Of her work, Rita Dove has written:

> In contrast to much of the poetry being written today—intellectualized lyricism characterized by an application of inductive thought to unusual images—Lucille Clifton's poems are compact and self-sufficient...Her revelations then resemble the epiphanies of childhood and early adolescence, when one's lack of preconceptions about the self allowed for brilliant slippage into the metaphysical, a glimpse into an egoless, utterly thingful and serene world.

Lucille Clifton's honors include an Emmy Award from the American Academy of Television Arts and Sciences, a Lannan Literary Award, two fellowships from the National Endowment for the Arts, the Shelley Memorial Award, the YM-YWHA Poetry Center Discovery Award, and the 2007 Ruth Lilly Prize. In 1999, she was elected a Chancellor of the Academy of American Poets. She has served as Poet Laureate for the State of Maryland and Distinguished Professor of Humanities at St. Mary's College of Maryland.

After a long battle with cancer, Lucille Clifton died on February 13, 2010, at the age of 73.

Taken from The Academy of American Poets Website, Poets.org.

Chard deNiord

Chard deNiord is the author of four books of poetry, *The Double Truth* (The University of Pittsburgh Press), *Night Mowing* (The University of Pittsburgh Press, 2005), *Sharp Golden Thorn* (Marsh Hawk Press, 2003), and *Asleep in the Fire* (University of Alabama Press, 1990). He is an associate professor of English at Providence College. He lives in Putney, Vermont with his wife Liz.